What are spreadsheets?

Spreadsheets are grids that help you to organize numbers and words into neat columns and rows. Microsoft® Excel 97 comes with some very useful **tools** that will help you to do things such as calculating what you spend, putting lists into alphabetical order and creating colourful charts and graphs. Here are some of the things that you can do using Microsoft® Excel 97:

You can create different type styles.

You can sort lists into alphabetical order.

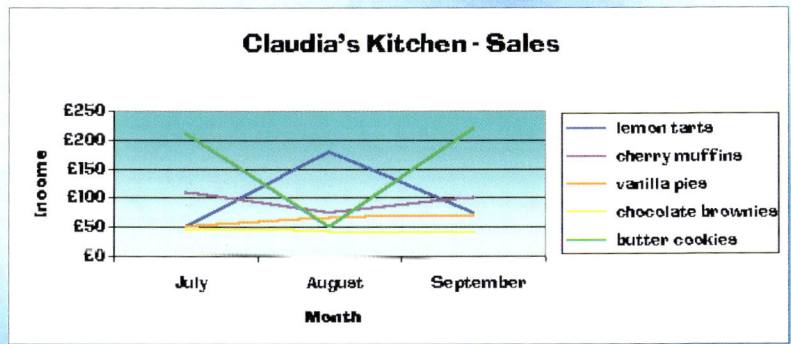

Claudia's Kitchen
Sales

	July	August	September	TOTAL
lemon tarts	£50	£180	£75	£305
cherry muffins	£110	£75	£100	£285
vanilla pies	£50	£65	£70	£185
chocolate brownies	£45	£42	£40	£127
butter cookies	£210	£50	£220	£480
TOTAL	£465	£412	£505	£1,382

Excel can do all sorts of sums for you, such as adding a row or a column of numbers.

If you change one of the numbers in a sum, the answer changes automatically.

The screen

You may find that your screen doesn't look quite the same as the ones in this book. This doesn't mean there's something wrong with your computer – computers can be set up with different colours and patterns.

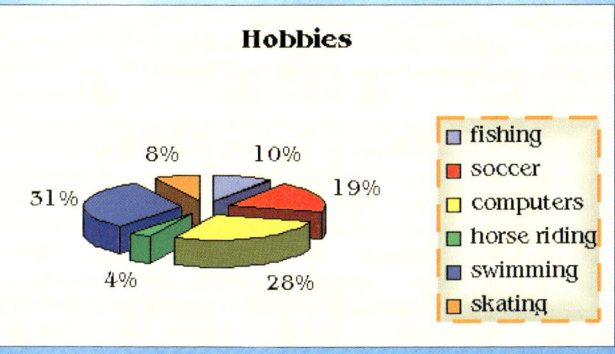

You can create graphs and charts like these using Excel.

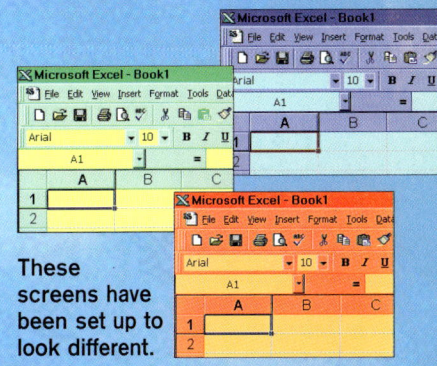

These screens have been set up to look different.

What do I need?

To use this book, you'll need a personal computer, or **PC**. There are other kinds of computers, but PCs are the ones most often used in homes and offices. A PC consists of several pieces of equipment. In computer jargon, this equipment is known as **hardware**. Most PCs look similar to the one on this page. You'll also need **software**. Software is the name for computer programs, which give your computer instructions.

This picture shows a PC. All PCs look slightly different. Yours may not look exactly like this one.

Hardware

This picture shows the hardware you will need.

The part which has a screen is called the monitor.

You use the CD-ROM drive to load software.

This is a mouse.

This is a printer. If you want to print what you do onto paper, you'll need a printer.

Keyboard

You may find the mouse easier to use if you put it on a mouse mat.

CD-ROM disc

The system unit contains parts that help your computer work. It includes the **hard disk drive**, where your computer stores information.

Software

Software usually comes on a disc, called a **CD-ROM**. You use the disc to load, or install, the software onto your computer. Once you have installed software onto your computer, the information stays there for you to use. You'll need two types of software. Your computer will probably already have Microsoft® Windows® 95 or 98 on it. This kind of software is called an operating system. It enables other software to work. You will also need Microsoft® Excel 97. Excel is available either on its own or as part of Microsoft® Office 97, which also contains other programs. To find out if Excel is already on your PC, turn to page 6.

Plugging in

Make sure that the keyboard, monitor, mouse, system unit and printer are connected to each other. Remember to plug the monitor, system unit and printer into the power supply.

Plugs should only be plugged into sockets of a similar shape.

This cable leads to the mouse.

This cable is plugged into the system unit and into the keyboard.

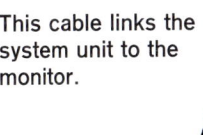

This cable links the system unit to the monitor.

This cable links the system unit to the printer.

Make sure that the other ends of these cables are plugged into the mains power supply.

Important

After you have switched on your computer (see below), you shouldn't just switch it off when you've finished using it. There are various things you need to do before you switch off, or you may find it difficult to switch on next time you use it.

See pages 56-57 for instructions on how to switch off the computer.

Switching on

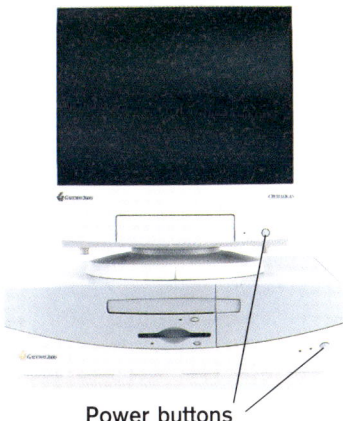

Power buttons

1. Press the power button on the system unit. If there is a power button on the monitor, press that too. Both parts need to be switched on.

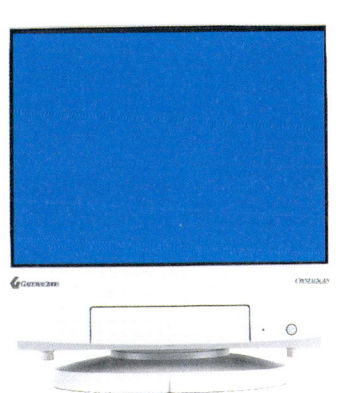

2. As the computer gets ready, it hums and the screen may flash. Some computers ask you for a password. If yours does, page 60 tells you what to do.

3. Wait for a while and don't press any buttons. When the screen looks something like this, it is ready to use. This is called the Windows® screen.

5

Do I have Microsoft® Excel 97?

Now that you've switched on the computer, you need to see if you have Microsoft® Excel 97. To do this, you need to learn how to use the mouse.

This is a computer mouse. Don't worry if yours looks different. It will work in a similar way.

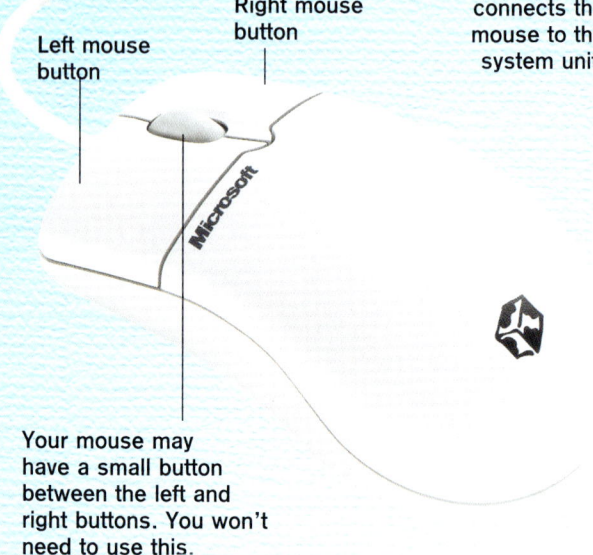

Left mouse button

Right mouse button

This cable connects the mouse to the system unit.

Using the mouse

1. Place the mouse on the mouse mat and rest your hand on the mouse. Your first finger should be on the left button. You'll use this button most of the time.

2. Move the mouse across the mat until you can see a white arrow on the computer's screen. The arrow is called the **pointer**. The pointer moves as you move the mouse around.

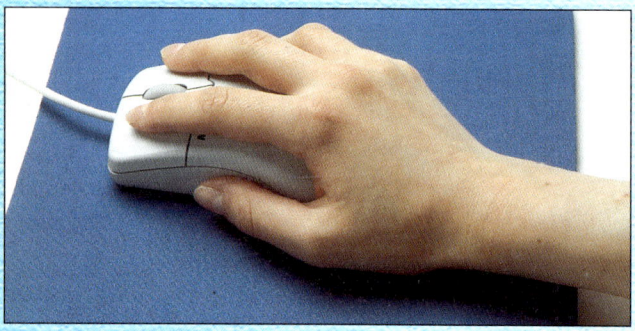

Your mouse may have a small button between the left and right buttons. You won't need to use this.

Mouse fact

People who don't know how a mouse works have sometimes been known to move them around on the monitor and to wave them in the air, like a television remote control.

3. Use your first finger to press and release the left button on the mouse. This is called **clicking**. Clicking is used when you want to tell the computer to do something.

Looking for Excel

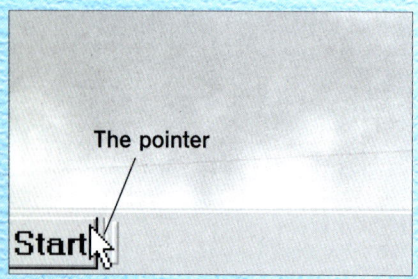

The pointer

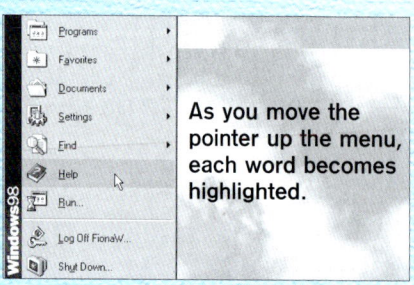

As you move the pointer up the menu, each word becomes highlighted.

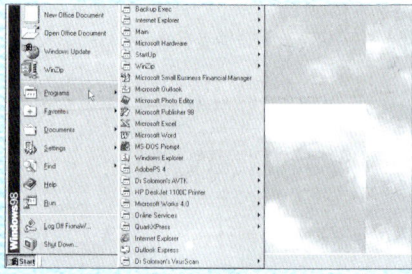

1. Move the pointer over Start in the corner of the screen. A message appears which reads 'Click here to begin'. Press the left mouse button to click.

2. A list, called a **menu**, appears. Move the pointer up the menu, until the word Programs is **highlighted**. Then, click the left mouse button.

3. Another menu appears. If Excel is on your computer, it should be beside a turquoise X. If it isn't there, page 61 shows you where else it might be.

Opening Microsoft® Excel 97

To open Microsoft® Excel 97, you need to choose it from the menu, using the mouse. Follow these steps:

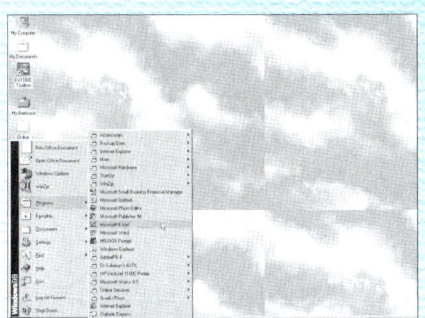

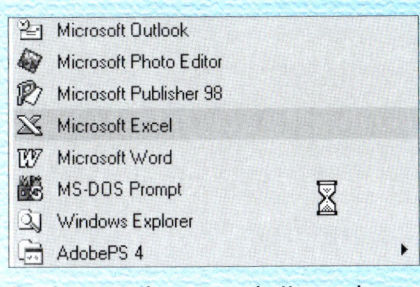

Don't press the mouse buttons when you see the egg-timer shape.

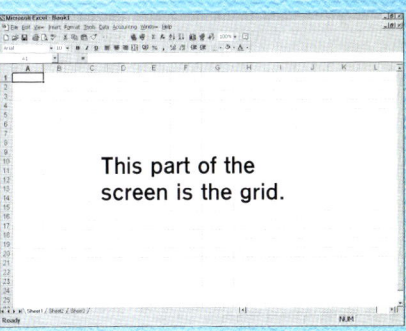

This part of the screen is the grid.

1. When you've found Excel, move the mouse to the right so that the pointer is over the second menu. Move the pointer over Excel, then click.

2. As you wait for your computer to find Excel, you may see the pointer change to an egg-timer shape. This means your computer is busy.

3. In a few seconds your screen will look like the one in this picture. This is the Microsoft® Excel 97 screen. See page 8 to find out about it.

Pointer shapes

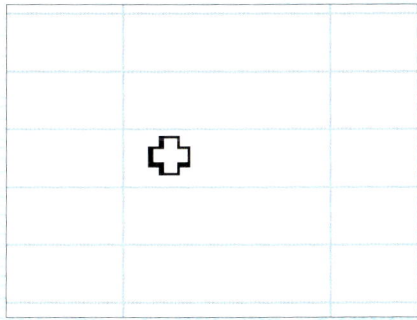

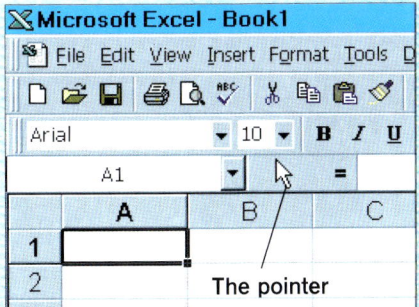

The pointer

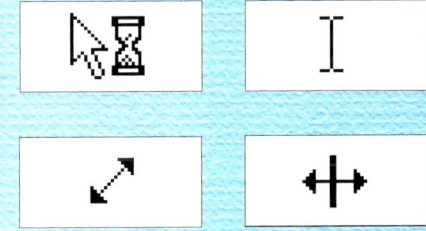

Here are some more pointer shapes you will see.

The pointer changes shape depending on where it is on the Microsoft® Excel 97 screen. When it is over the grid, the pointer becomes a cross.

If you move the pointer over some of the areas at the top and the bottom of the screen, the pointer changes to an arrow shape again.

As you use Excel, you will notice more pointer shapes (a few are shown above). These will be explained in the book as you need to use them.

Before Microsoft® Excel 97

Before spreadsheet programs, such as Excel, were developed, most people wrote calculations on large pieces of paper. This kind of paper, called ledger paper, is divided into little squares, like the grid on your screen. It is far quicker and easier to use spreadsheets on your computer.

Exploring the Excel screen

Your screen will now look similar to the one below. The grid area is part of an Excel spreadsheet. Spreadsheets are sometimes called worksheets.

Don't let this confuse you – spreadsheets and worksheets are the same thing. The pictures and words at the top of the screen are called tools. Tools help you do things such as creating charts and doing sums. Here is a tour of the screen:

The words and pictures represent tools. You will learn to use some of them in this book.

The grid area in the middle of the screen is part of a spreadsheet.

These are called **columns**. Each column has a letter.

The rows of tools are called **toolbars**. If some are missing from your screen, page 60 shows you how you can find them.

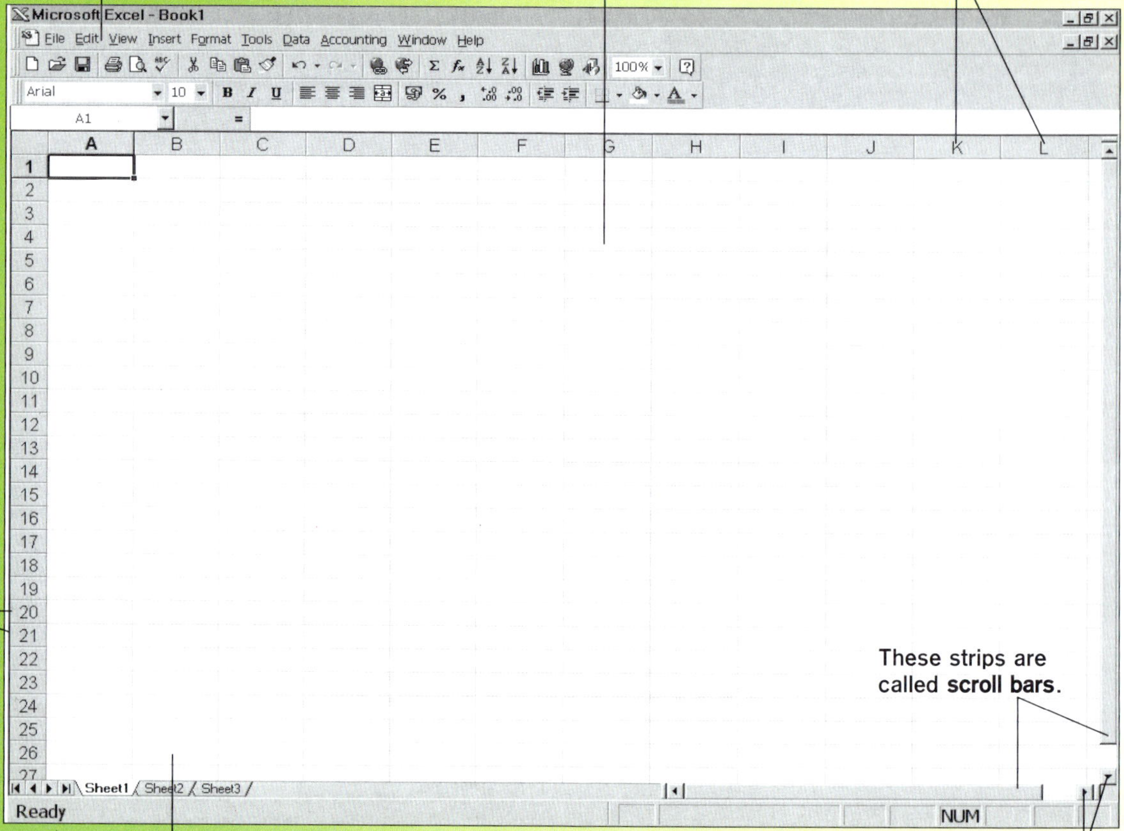

These are called **rows**. Each row has a number.

These strips are called **scroll bars**.

You type in the little boxes called **cells**. You'll see the word 'cell' a lot in this book.

You can click on the arrow at each end of the scroll bars to see more cells.

Finding your way around

When you open Microsoft® Excel 97, you only see the top left-hand corner of a spreadsheet. A whole spreadsheet has 65,636 rows and 256 columns – that means 16,802,816 cells! You can find out how to use the scroll bars to see more of the cells on a spreadsheet on page 13.

To help you find particular cells, you can refer to them by using their column letter, followed by their row number – like map coordinates. For example, the cell in the third row down in column C is called C3.

Starting to type

Follow these simple steps to find out how to use the letter keys in the middle of the keyboard to type small letters (lower case). You can find out more about the keyboard on pages 10-11.

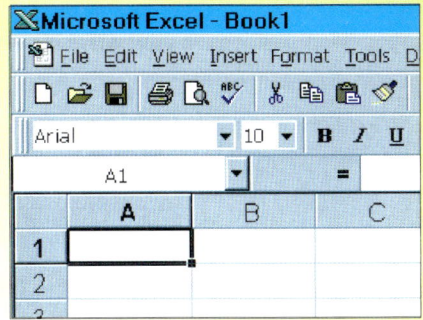

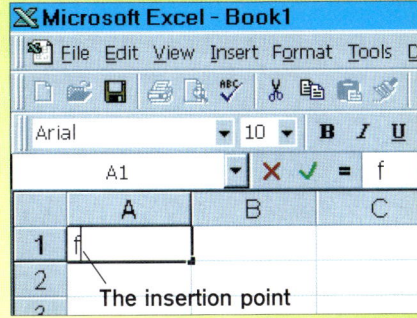

The insertion point

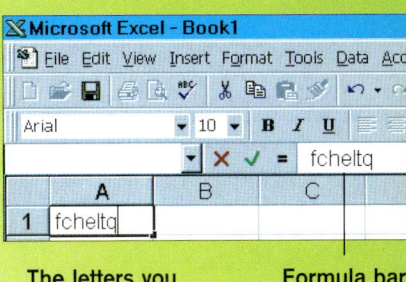

The letters you type appear in the active cell.

Formula bar

1. Cell A1 has a bold line around it. This is called the **active cell**. Press a letter key on the keyboard, lightly. The letter appears in the active cell.

2. As the letter appears, a flashing line appears to its right. This is called the **insertion point**. It shows you where you can type more letters.

3. Press a few more letter keys, one at a time. As the letters appear in the active cell, they also appear at the top of the spreadsheet in the **formula bar**.

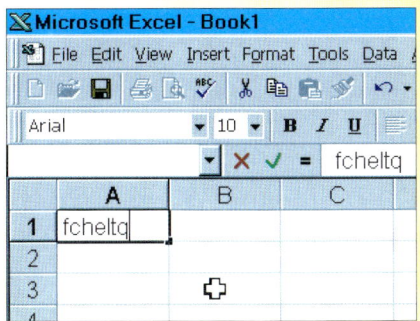

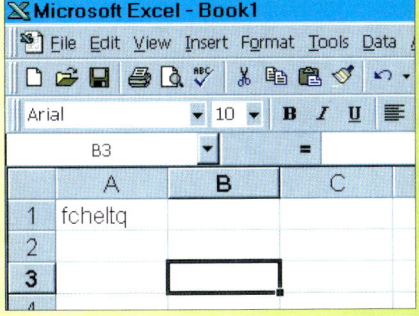

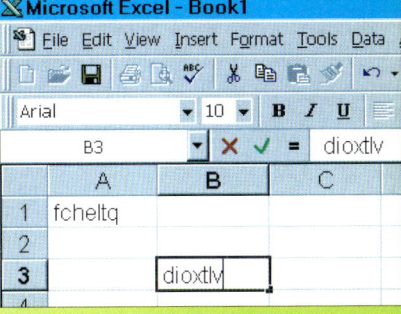

4. To type in another cell, you have to make it active. Move the mouse so the cross-shaped pointer is over cell B3. Click the left mouse button once.

5. A bold line appears around cell B3 and disappears from cell A1. The letters you typed in cell A1 remain, but they disappear from the formula bar.

6. Press some more letter keys. Cell B3 is now the active cell. The letters you type appear in that cell and in the formula bar at the top of the spreadsheet.

The Office Assistant

You may see an animated picture in a box on your screen. This is called the Office Assistant. You can ask the Assistant for help (see page 61), but its instructions can be confusing. To make the Assistant disappear for now, move the pointer over the cross in the corner of the box and click.

Exploring the keyboard

You may have noticed that the letter keys are jumbled up in the middle of the keyboard. As you work your way through the book, you'll find out what the other keys are, surrounding them. You won't need them all, but here are some you will find useful.

This is the Shift key. You can use this to type capital letters and some of the signs.

You can use the Caps Lock key to make all the letters capitals.

The Backspace key removes the last thing you typed.

The Enter, or Return, key tells your computer to carry out an instruction.

The **Delete** key removes words and sentences.

The Ctrl and Alt keys help you give your computer instructions.

Press the Space bar to put a gap between words and numbers.

Use this key to type a colon or a semi-colon.

Another Shift key

The arrow keys help you to move around the screen (see below).

Moving around

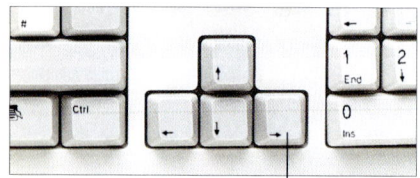

Press this key.

1. Look for the arrow keys on the keyboard. Press the right arrow key once, lightly. Watch what happens to the spreadsheet on your screen.

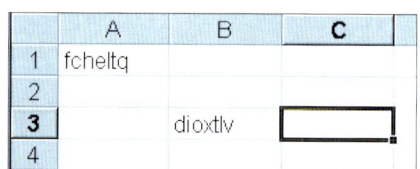

2. The next cell to the right becomes the active cell (a bold line appears around it). Press some letter keys. They will appear in the active cell.

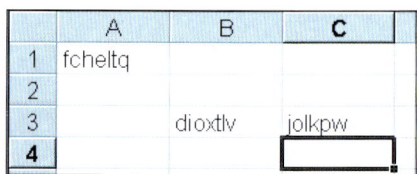

3. Now press the key with the arrow pointing down. The next cell down becomes active. Try pressing the other arrow keys too and watch what happens.

Typing your name

Follow these steps to find out how to use the keyboard to type capital letters and spaces.

1. Move to a new cell. You can either use arrow keys, or use the mouse to move the pointer over the cell you want, then click the left mouse button.

2. To type a capital letter, hold down one of the Shift keys and press the first letter of your name. A single capital letter appears in the active cell.

3. Take your finger off the Shift key and type the rest of your name in lower case letters. If you make a mistake, press the Backspace key.

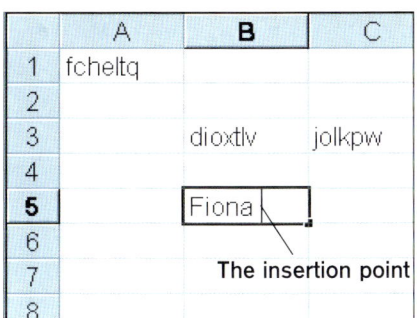

4. To make a gap before you type your surname, press the Space bar once, so the insertion point moves one space to the right.

5. Type your surname. Don't worry if the letters you type spill into the next cell. Press the Enter key when you have finished typing in the cell.

Tip

If you want to type in just capital letters, press the Caps Lock key. Press some letter keys. To type lower case letters, just press the Caps Lock key again.

The Shift keys

As well as using the Shift keys to type capital letters, you can use them to type the signs that are on some of the keys. Hold down one of the Shift keys, and press one of the keys with two signs on. The sign at the top of the key appears on the screen.

If the key is pressed on its own, the lower sign appears on the screen. If Shift is held down as the key is pressed, the upper sign appears.

1. Making a simple address list

These pages show you how to make a simple address list. You can add as many addresses as you like and add extra information too, such as your friends' phone numbers or e-mail addresses.

Clearing the screen

1. To clear the screen, first press Enter. Hold down the Ctrl key while you press the letter A on the keyboard.

2. Press Delete to remove all the letters you have typed. Then make the screen white again by clicking once in any cell.

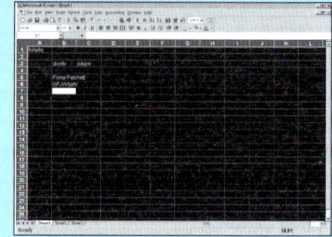

Letters go white on a black background, except in the last cell you clicked on.

Typing the headings

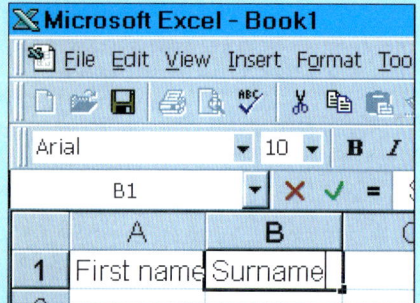

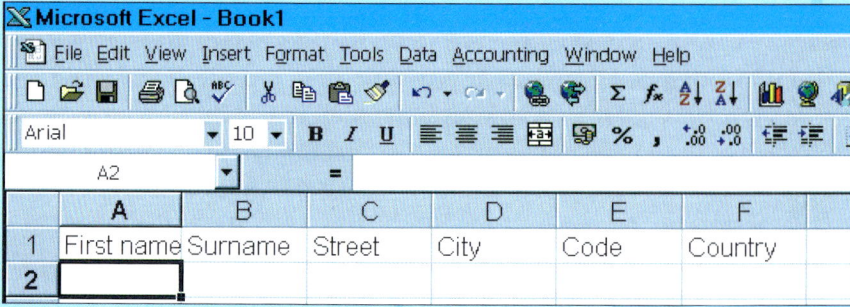

1. Move the pointer over cell A1. Press the left mouse button to click. Type 'First name'. Press the right arrow key once, then type 'Surname' in cell B1.

2. Press the right arrow key again and type 'Street'. Continue until you have typed all the headings that you want in your address list.

3. Use the arrow keys to move to cell A2. Type someone's first name. Type their details into each cell along row 2. See the steps below to widen columns.

Widening columns

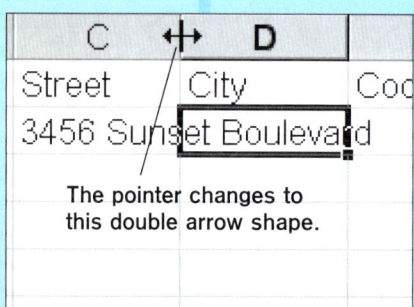

The pointer changes to this double arrow shape.

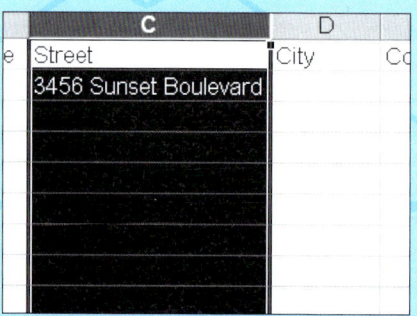

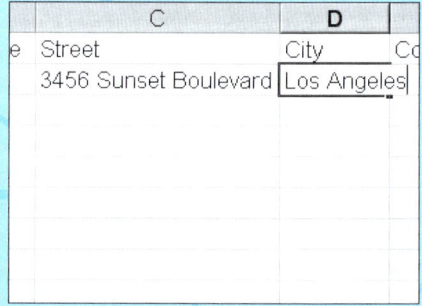

1. To widen a column, first move to the next cell. Move the pointer over the right-hand edge of the box at the top of the column you want to widen.

2. Press the left mouse button twice very quickly. This is called **double-clicking**. The column will widen to fit in everything you have typed.

3. If the column goes black, click in the next cell you want to type in, to make it white again. Carry on typing until you've filled in all the details.

One step ahead

As you work, Microsoft® Excel 97 tries to guess what you want to write. Computers are clever, but they don't always get things right...

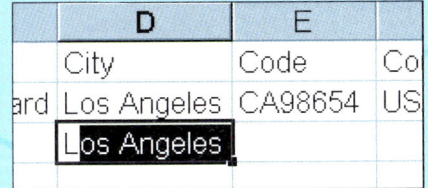
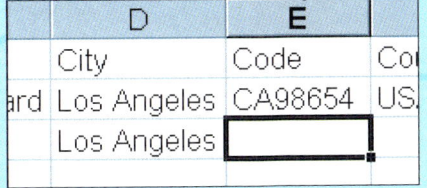
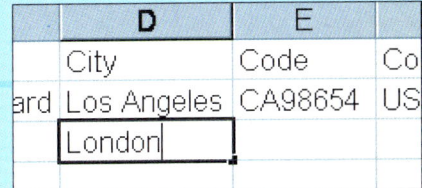

1. If the first few letters you type match a word you have already typed in that column, Excel guesses that you want to type it again and completes it for you.

2. This can be helpful if Excel gets it right. If you are happy with the guess, press the right arrow key on the keyboard to move to the next cell.

3. If you were going to type something different, ignore Excel and type the letters you want. The word that Microsoft® Excel 97 guessed disappears.

Using more rows

1. If you fill all the rows on the screen, press the down arrow key. A new row appears at the bottom of the screen and the top row disappears.

2. To see the rows at the top of the list again, move the pointer over the small, black arrow at the top of the vertical scroll bar and click on it.

3. If you want to go back to the rows further down the spreadsheet, click on the small, black arrow at the bottom of the vertical scroll bar.

4. If you want to use more columns than you can see on your screen, click on the arrows at each end of the horizontal scroll bar to see columns to the left and right.

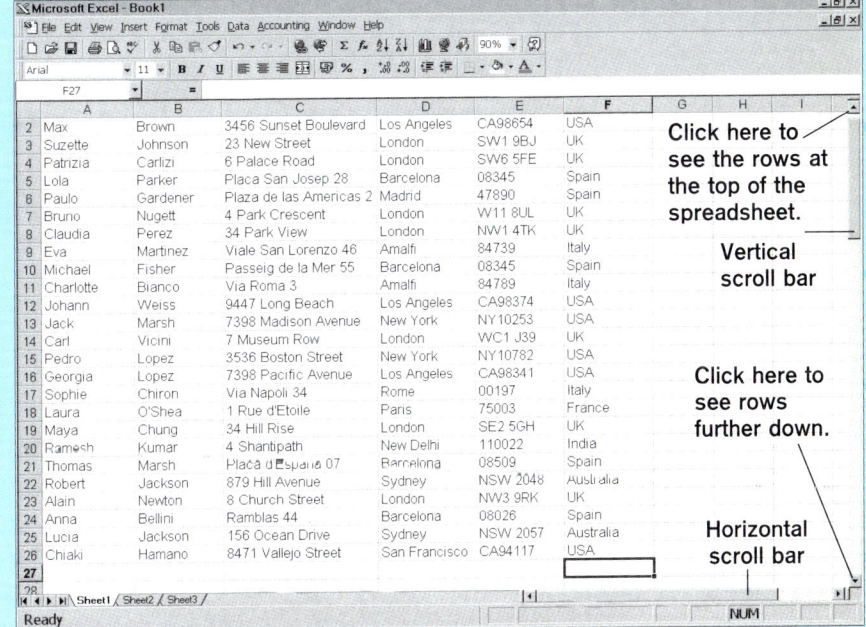

Important

When you type a lot of information into a spreadsheet, you should **save** what you have done so you can come back to it another time. See pages 14-15 to find out about saving.

2. Saving what I've done

Before you type too much, you will need to save what you have done. When you save a spreadsheet, you store it on your computer's hard disk drive. This means you can switch off your computer and come back to your work another time.

If you store spreadsheets in a folder, they will be easier to find.

Creating your own folder

Everything that is stored on your hard disk drive is divided into groups, called **folders**. The first time you save some work, you will need to create your own folder within a ready-made folder, called **My Documents**. Each time you save a new spreadsheet, you can store it in your folder. This makes it easier to find your work again.

This box is called the Save As box.

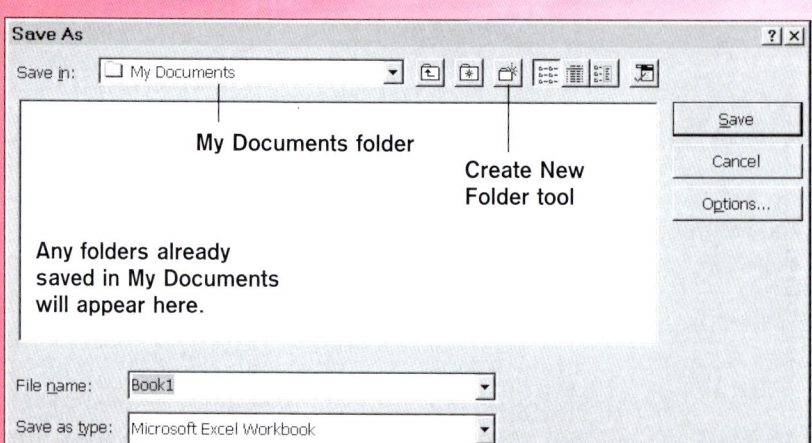

Save tool

1. To create a folder, move the pointer over the Save tool on one of the toolbars near the top of the screen. Click on it. The Save As box appears on your screen (see above right).

2. Beside the words Save in at the top of the box, you will see the name of a folder called My Documents. The folder you create will be saved within the My Documents folder.

3. At the top of the Save As box, you will see three yellow symbols. The symbol with a star shape behind it is called the Create New Folder tool. Click on it.

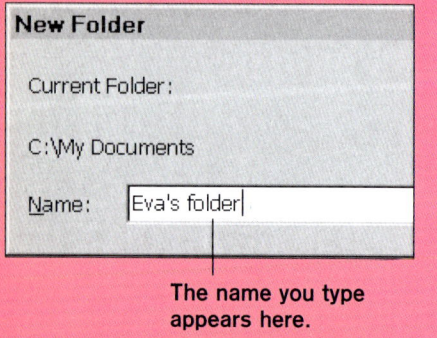

The name you type appears here.

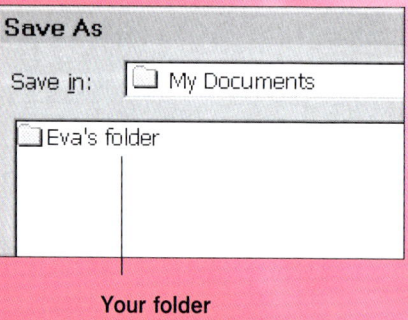

Your folder

4. The New Folder box pops up with the words New Folder in the white area. Type a name for your folder that will be easy to remember. The name you type will replace New Folder.

5. Move the pointer over OK on the right-hand side of the box and click. The New Folder box disappears. If you look in the main part of the Save As box, you will see your folder.

Tip

As you use this book, you will sometimes see highlighted lettering (it appears on a dark background). Any letters you type will replace these letters. You don't have to press Delete to remove them first.

How to save

This section shows you how to save your address list spreadsheet in the folder you have just created. When you save a spreadsheet, Microsoft® Excel 97 calls it a **file**. This is just more jargon, so don't let it confuse you.

 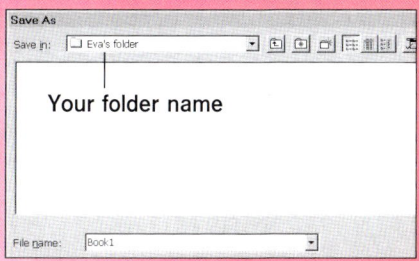 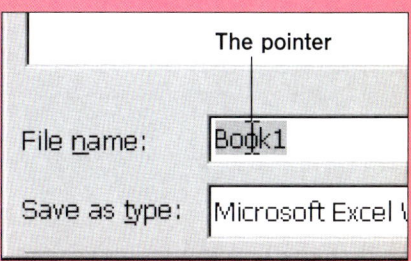

1. Move the pointer over your folder in the main part of the box and click the left mouse button. Now click on Open on the right-hand side of the box.

2. Your folder name will appear next to Save in. Beside File name, you will see Book1. This is the name Excel gives your spreadsheet before you save it.

3. Move the pointer over Book1. The pointer becomes a vertical line. Double-click to highlight Book1. It appears on a dark background.

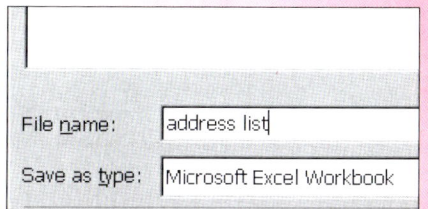 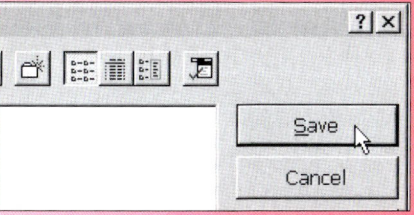 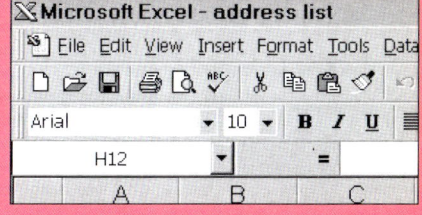

4. Type a new name for the spreadsheet that will be easy to remember. It's best to choose something that describes what you have typed.

5. Move the pointer over the word Save on the right-hand side of the box. Click the mouse button once. Your spreadsheet is saved.

6. The name you typed replaces Book1 in the top left-hand corner of the screen. If you want to switch off your computer, turn to pages 56-57.

More about saving

You can save as many spreadsheets as you like in your folder. When you want to save your next spreadsheet, click once on the Save tool to make the Save As box appear. Then just follow steps 1-6 above. Each spreadsheet you save will need a different name.

If you have already saved a spreadsheet, just click once on the Save tool to save any changes you have made. The Save As box doesn't appear because you have already given the spreadsheet a name. If you want to give the new version another name, page 25 shows you how.

There is often more than one way to tell your computer to do something. Instead of clicking on the Save tool, you can hold down the Ctrl key and press the letter S key to save.

3. Correcting mistakes

You may look at your address list and spot a few mistakes or someone on your list may move and change address, so it's very useful to know how to change what you have typed.

Change a few letters

1. Move the pointer over the cell you want to change. Double-click by quickly pressing the left mouse button twice. The cell becomes active.

2. An insertion point appears inside the cell. Use the arrow keys to move the insertion point so it is to the left of the letters you want to remove.

Insertion point

3. Press the Delete key once. One letter to the right of the insertion point disappears. To delete more letters, press the Delete key again.

4. When you have deleted all the letters you need to, you can type in the correct ones. They will appear where the insertion point flashes.

5. When you are happy with the changes you have made in the cell, press the Enter key. Remember to click on the Save tool to save these changes.

Change a whole cell

If you want to remove everything you have typed from more than one cell, you can follow the steps on the opposite page.

If you want to remove everything you have typed in just one cell, you can use the Delete key to remove it all in one go. Follow these two steps to find out how.

1. Move the pointer over the cell that you want to change. Then, click the left mouse button once.

2. Press the Delete key. All the letters in the cell disappear. Type the correct letters, then press the Enter key.

Selecting areas to delete

Follow these steps to find out how to choose, or **select**, several cells and delete what is inside them all in one go. Selecting cells is very useful – you will need to select cells in lots of the projects in this book.

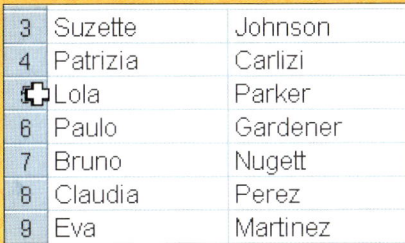

1. To select a whole row and delete it, move the pointer over the number at the end of the row. The pointer should be a cross shape.

The background of the first cell you select remains white.

2. Press the left mouse button to click on the row number. The row is selected when all the cells, except the first one, appear on a black background.

Click on any cell to remove the black background.

3. Press Delete to remove the letters. You can also delete the letters in a column. Click on the letter at the top of the column to select it. Then, press Delete.

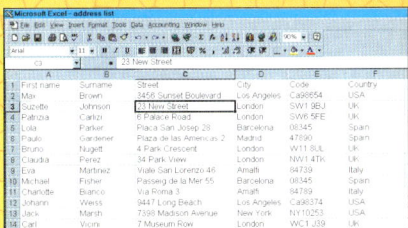

4. To select just a few cells, move the pointer over the first cell you want to delete. Press the left mouse button and hold it down.

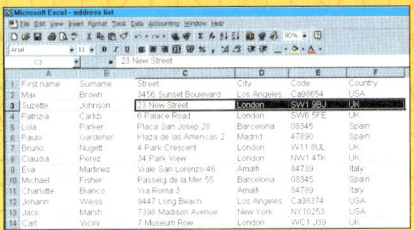

5. Move the mouse so the pointer moves to the right. When all the cells you want to delete are selected, release the mouse button.

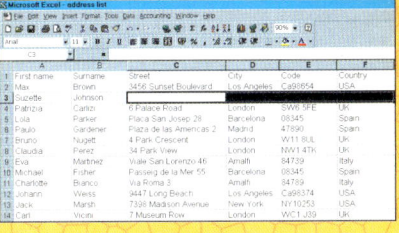

6. Just press the Delete key and the letters in the selected cells will disappear. Click once in any cell to remove the black background.

Tip

Sooner or later you may delete the wrong thing. If you change your mind about the last thing you deleted, you can easily get it back on your screen. Before you do anything else, click on the Undo tool on the toolbar. The letters you deleted reappear.

Undo tool

Keep saving

After you have made any changes to your work, you should save your work again. Just click on the Save tool once. Any changes you have made will be saved automatically. When you work, remember to click on the Save tool regularly.

Save tool

If someone switches off your computer, you will lose any work that you haven't saved.

4. Printing onto paper

If you have a printer, you can print your spreadsheets onto paper. First of all, connect your printer to the power supply. Switch on the printer's power button, which is probably on the front of the printer. Remember to put some paper into the printer's paper tray.

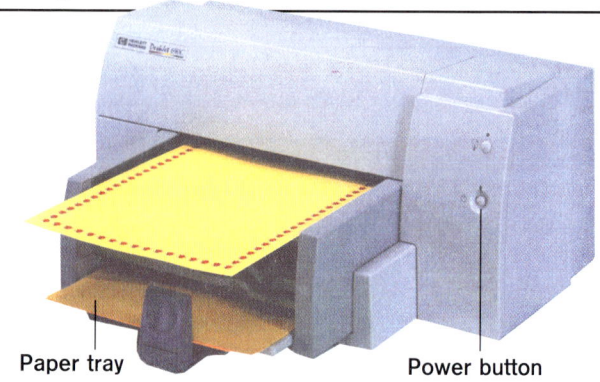

Paper tray   Power button

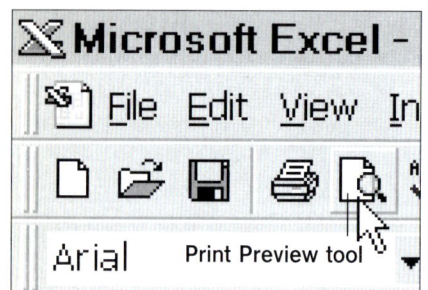

1. The spreadsheet you want to print should be on your screen. To find out how it will look on paper, click on the Print Preview tool.

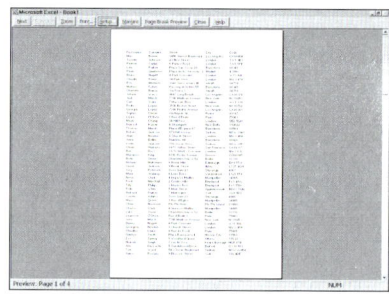

2. A small version of the page appears. The grid lines don't appear because they will not print. Page 50 shows you how to add grid lines that will print.

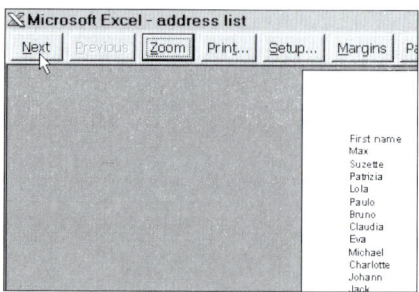

3. If you have typed lots of rows, they may spill onto another page. Click on the word Next near the top of the screen to see the next page.

Part of the Page Setup box.

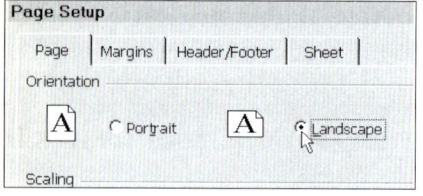

4. If the columns don't fit across the page, you could try turning the page on its side (see right). Click on Setup. The Page Setup box appears. Click on Landscape, then press Enter.

5. To turn the page back to how it was, click on Setup, then on Portrait. Press Enter. When you are happy with the way your spreadsheet looks on the page, click on Close.

Print Preview screen

When the page is on its side, like this, it is called landscape.

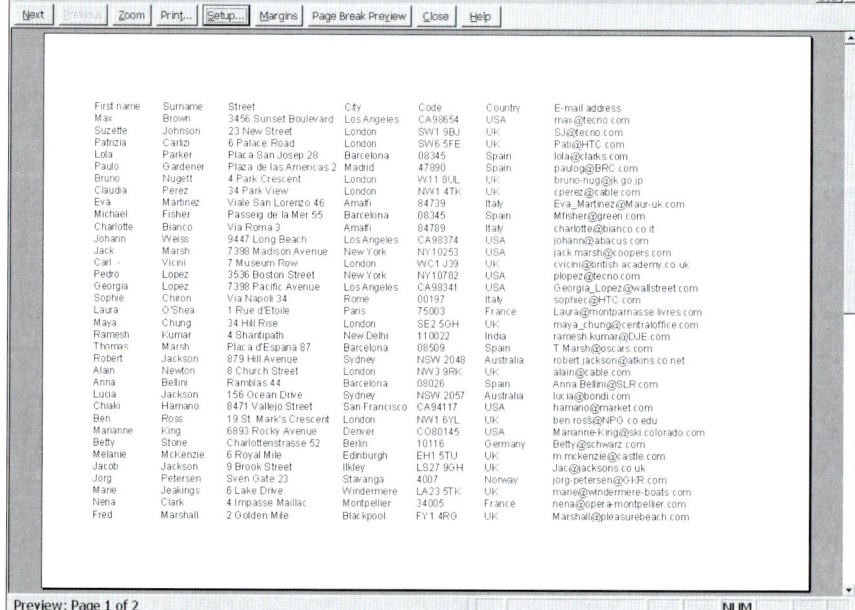

One copy

It is always a good idea to print one copy before printing more, so that if you spot a mistake, you will still have a chance to correct it without wasting lots of pieces of paper.

To print one copy of your work, click on the Print tool, at the top of the screen. A few seconds later, your work will print.

Printing more copies

Once you are happy with what you have printed, you can print as many copies as you like.

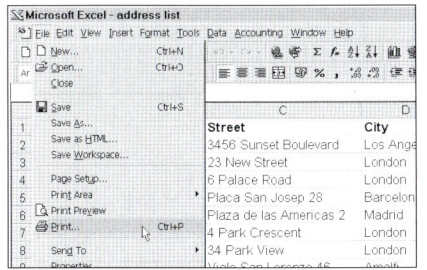

The Print box

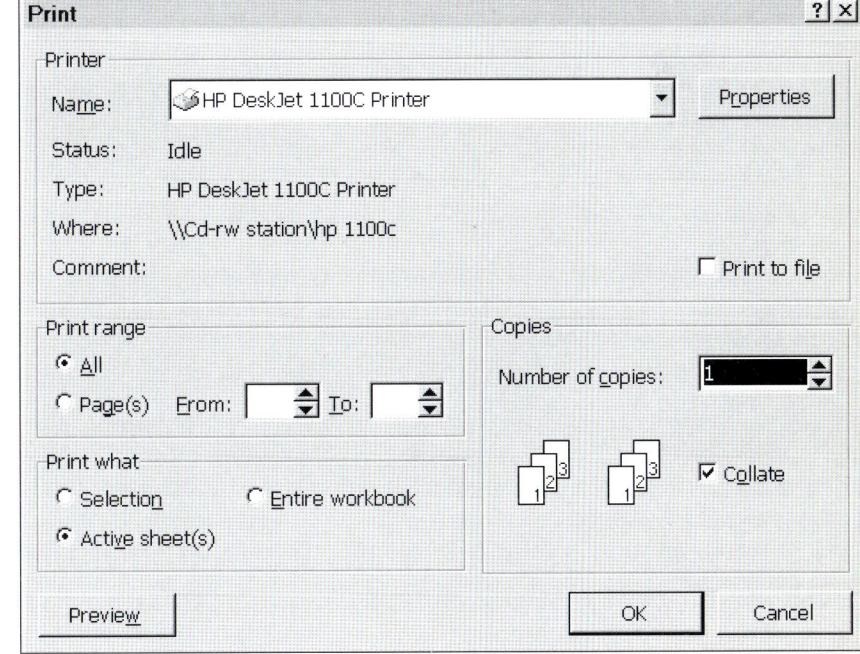

1. Click on File at the top of the screen. On the menu, click on Print. The Print box appears (see right). Find the box beside Number of copies.

2. Type the number of copies you want to print. The number you type will appear in this box. Click on OK at the bottom of the box. Your work will print.

The page on the left is portrait and the page below is landscape.

Tip

There's a really quick way to make the Print box appear on the screen, without using the mouse. Hold down the Ctrl key and press the letter P. The Print box will appear.

5. Adding two numbers

Excel is very useful if you want to do any kind of sums. The example on these pages shows you how to add the number of ice creams sold in two different months, but you can add any two numbers together in the same way. On the next few pages in this book, you will also find out how to use Microsoft® Excel 97 to subtract, multiply and divide numbers.

A new spreadsheet

To **close** the last spreadsheet you used, follow the steps on page 56. To open a new spreadsheet, click on the New tool at the top of the screen. The New tool looks a bit like a piece of paper with the corner turned over. A new spreadsheet appears.

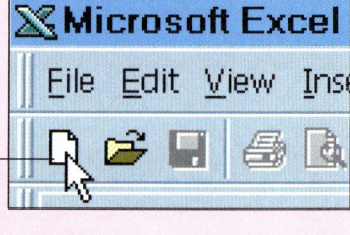

The New tool

Typing numbers

This appears in capital letters.

The pointer changes to this double arrow shape.

1. Press the right arrow key to move to cell B1. Type a month of the year. Press the right arrow key again to move to cell C1. Type the next month.

2. Use the arrow key to move to cell D1. Press the Caps Lock key. Type 'TOTAL'. Press Caps Lock again. The next letters you type will be lower case.

3. Move to cell A2 and type the first item you want to add. To make the column wider, double-click on the edge of the box at the top of column A.

4. Move to cell B2 and type a number. This example shows the number of strawberry ice creams that were sold in the month of July.

5. Move to cell C2 and type a number for the second month. Use the arrow keys to move down to cell A3 and type another item.

6. Press the right arrow key to move to cell B3. Type a number for the first month. In cell C3, type a number for the second month. Press Enter.

Adding the numbers

To add using Microsoft® Excel 97, you have to write a set of instructions, called a **formula**, which tells your computer which numbers to add. The following steps show you how to write a formula that adds two numbers in the same row.

	B	C	D
	July	August	TOTAL
	354	665	=
	265	529	

1. Click in cell D2. This is where the answer will appear. Type an equals sign. This tells your computer that you are going to type a formula.

	A	B	C	D
1		July	August	TOTAL
2	Strawberry ice creams	354	665	=B2
3	Vanilla ice creams	265	529	

2. Instead of typing the first number you want to add, type the coordinates of the cell that contains the number. In this case, type B2.

	B	C	D
	July	August	TOTAL
	354	665	=B2+
	265	529	

3. Hold down the Shift key and press the key with the equals sign and the plus sign on. The plus sign appears in cell D2. Release the Shift key.

	B	C	D
	July	August	TOTAL
	354	665	=B2+C2
	265	529	

4. Type the coordinates of the cell containing the second number you want to add. In this case, type C2. Then press the Enter key.

	B	C	D
	July	August	TOTAL
	354	665	1019
	265	529	=B3+C3

5. The answer to the formula appears in cell D2. To find the total for the second row, type an equals sign in cell D3, then follow steps 2, 3 and 4.

	B	C	D
	July	August	TOTAL
	354	665	1019
	265	529	794

6. If you want to add lots of rows at once, see page 22. To save your work, click on the Save tool, then see steps 1-6 on page 15.

See pages 48-49 to change the lettering style.

	JULY	AUGUST	TOTAL
STRAWBERRY ICE CREAMS	354	665	1019
VANILLA ICE CREAMS	265	529	

Page 50 shows you how to add grid lines that will print.

	April	May	TOTAL
		6685	13041
Visitors to museum	6356	7475	17219
Visitors to cathedral	9744		

Page 54 shows you how to line up words and numbers in each column.

6. Repeating a formula

If you have a long list of sums to do, you don't have to type a formula each time. This page shows a trick you can use to add lots of rows quickly.

Typing more rows

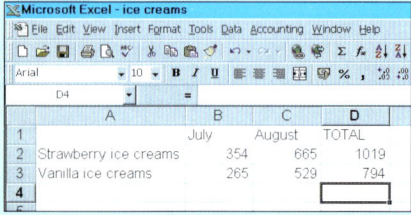

1. Make sure the spreadsheet where you added two numbers is on your screen. If you have saved and closed it, page 57 shows you how to reopen it.

2. Use the arrow keys to move to cell A4, then continue typing in more items and numbers on your list. You don't have to do any sums yet.

Adding the totals

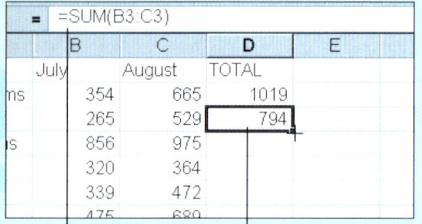

Formula bar — Click on cell D3.

1. Click on cell D3 where the total for row 3 appears. You can see the formula for this row in the formula bar, at the top of the screen.

Small, black square

2. Look in the bottom right-hand corner of cell D3. You will see a small, black square. Move the pointer over the square.

The pointer

3. As you move the pointer over the small, black square, the cross becomes thinner. Press the left mouse button and hold it down.

The adding formula has been repeated.

4. Move the mouse so the pointer moves down column D until there is a dotted line around all the cells where you want answers to appear.

5. Release the left mouse button. The total for each row appears in column D. Remove the black background by clicking on any cell.

7. Doing quick sums

This page shows you a very quick way to add a few numbers together, so the total appears at the bottom of the screen. The total won't actually appear on the spreadsheet, but if you want it to, follow the steps on page 26.

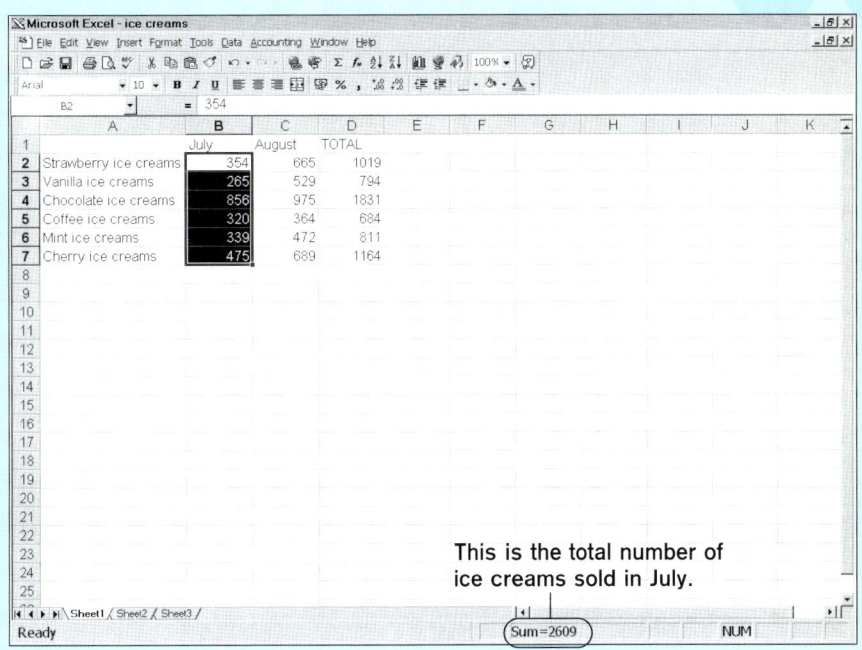

This is the total number of ice creams sold in July.

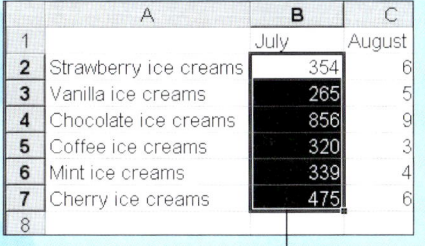

These cells are selected.

1. Move the pointer over cell B2. Press the left mouse button and hold it down while you move the pointer over the last number in column B.

2. Release the mouse button. On the strip below the horizontal scroll bar is the word Sum and an equals sign, followed by the total.

3. When you have read the total, click in any cell to remove the black background from the column. The total disappears too.

More sums

You can select any group of cells and find the total in the same way. Follow these steps to add two columns of numbers instead of one.

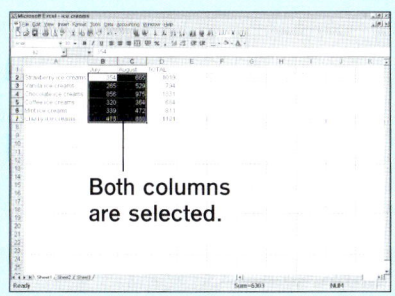

Both columns are selected.

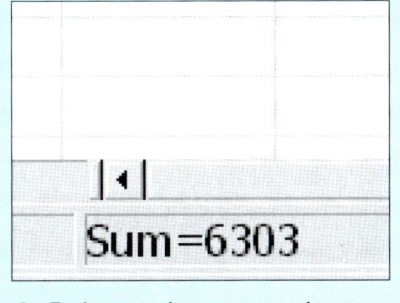

1. Move the pointer over cell B2. Press the left mouse button and hold it down while you move the pointer over the last number in column C.

2. Release the mouse button. The total of the numbers in both columns appears. You can find the total of more columns in the same way.

8. Typing different currencies

These pages show you how to include a currency sign with the numbers you type, so you can make a list of how much different items cost. Microsoft® Excel 97 can add signs for Dollars, Lire and even Chilean Pesos.

Making the list

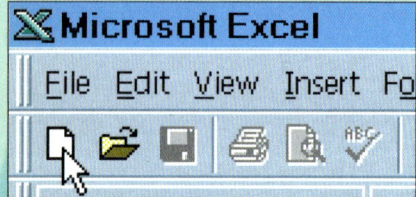

Click on the New tool.

1. Before you start, make sure you save and close any other spreadsheets you have used. Open a new spreadsheet by clicking on the New tool.

Widen column A if you need to.

2. In cell A1, type the heading 'Item'. Use the right arrow key to move to cell B1 and type the heading 'Amount'. In cell A2, type an item you have bought.

3. In cell B2, type how much the item cost, such as 1.50. Press the full stop key to type a decimal point. You don't need to type the currency sign yet.

4. Move to cell A3. If the number you typed ends in zero, don't worry that the zero disappears. You will find out later how to make it reappear.

Remember the decimal point.

5. In cell A3, type another item. In cell B3, type how much it cost. If, for example, the item cost 67 pence, type a decimal point before the 67.

6. Move to cell A4 and type the next item you bought. Type how much it cost in cell B4. Continue until you have typed everything you have bought.

Item	Amount
CD	£12.90
birthday card	£1.50
wrapping paper	£0.99
ribbon	£0.52
train fare	£3.20
red shoes	£25.00
earrings	£14.99
sandwich	£2.35
newspaper	£0.35
book	£6.99

Item	Amount
strawberries	$1.50
apples	$0.67
pears	$0.44
bananas	$0.70
cherries	$1.78
plums	$0.85
apricots	$0.52
oranges	$0.68
grapes	$1.25
raspberries	$2.15

Item	Amount
suntan lotion	69.00F
bikini	240.00F
sunglasses	135.00F
sarong	150.00F
book	129.00F
salad	40.00F
ice cream	25.00F
sunhat	140.00F

Adding the currency sign

These steps show you how to add a currency sign to all the prices in your list. Excel has most of the world's currency signs for you to choose from.

Click here.

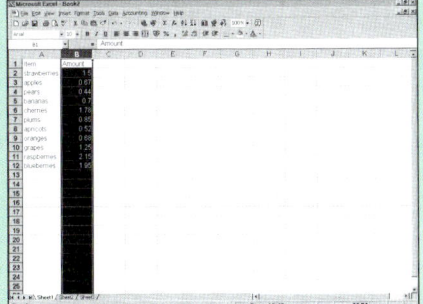 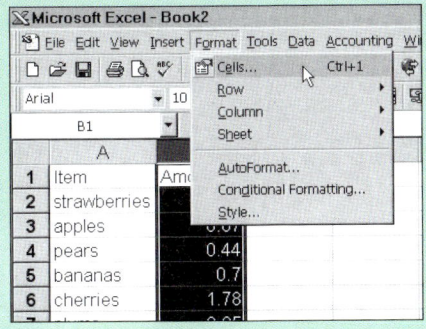 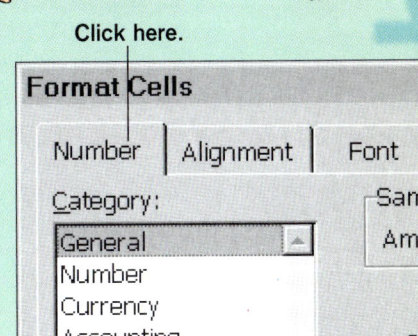

1. Select column B by clicking on the capital letter B at the top of the column. The lettering in column B will go white on a black background.

2. Click on the word Format near the top of the screen. A menu drops down. Move the pointer down the menu until Cells is highlighted, then click.

3. The Format Cells box appears on your screen (see more below). Move the pointer over the word Number at the top of the box and click on it.

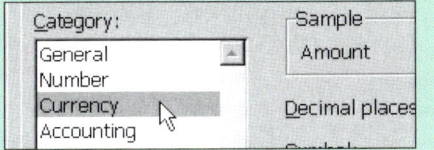

4. On the list below Category, move the pointer over the word Currency and click. Some more boxes will appear to the right of the list.

5. There should be a 2 in the Decimal places box to show that there will be two numbers after the decimal point. Click on the arrows until a 2 shows.

6. Click on the white box below the word Symbol so that a menu drops down. This menu shows the names and signs for different currencies.

7. Click on the arrows beside the menu to see more currencies. When you find the currency you want, move the pointer over its sign and click.

The Format Cells box will look like this after step 6.

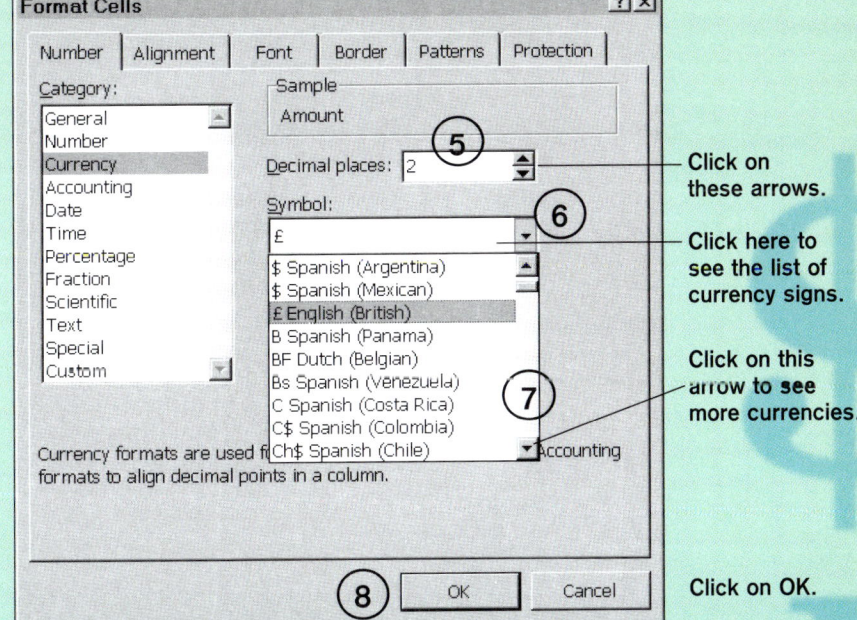

Click on these arrows.

Click here to see the list of currency signs.

Click on this arrow to see more currencies.

8. Click on OK. The Format Cells box disappears. If you want to see how much you've spent in that currency, look at the bottom of the screen.

Click on OK.

9. Click on any cell to remove the black background. Remember to save and close your spreadsheet when you have finished.

9. Adding a list of numbers

If you want to add a list of numbers so the total appears in one of the cells on your spreadsheet, you can use another of the tools on your screen. This tool is called the **AutoSum** tool. You won't need to type a formula as you did on page 21, because the AutoSum tool does it automatically for you. Click on the New tool to start a new spreadsheet.

Automatic adding

Widen column A if you need to.

1. In cell A1, type 'Item'. Move down column A, typing in items that you spend money on in one week. Then type 'TOTAL' in capital letters.

2. In B1, type 'Amount'. Move down column B, typing in how much each item cost. See page 25 to add currency signs to the numbers in column B.

3. Click in the cell beside 'TOTAL'. Move the pointer over the AutoSum tool on the toolbar and click. It looks a little like a capital letter E.

AutoSum tool

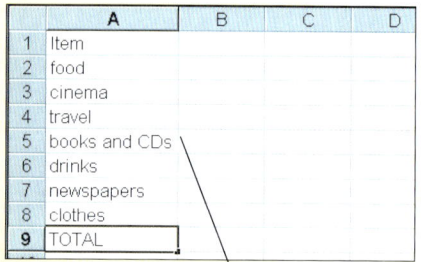

A formula appears in this cell.

4. A flashing, dotted line appears around the cells containing the numbers you are adding. A formula appears in the cell beside TOTAL.

Colon sign

5. Instead of a plus sign, this formula has a colon sign. The colon means that all the numbers in column B, from cell B2 to cell B8, will be added.

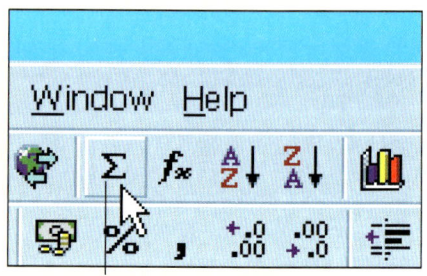

This is the total amount you've spent.

6. Press Enter. The total appears in the cell you clicked in. Save the list in your folder. Give it an appropriate name, such as 'spending - week 1'.

Tip

When you add currency signs to a whole column (see page 25), any new number in that column will appear with the currency sign and the same number of decimal places.

Adding numbers in a row

To add a row of numbers, click on the empty cell at the end of the row. Click on the AutoSum tool, then press Enter.

The total of the numbers in the cells from A1 to C1 appear in this cell.

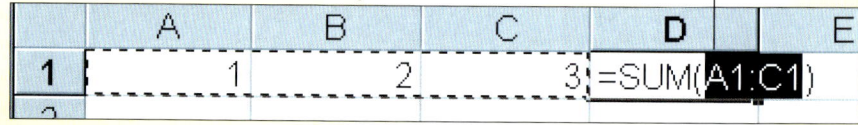

10. Changing prices

Some weeks you may spend far more than usual, or far less. When you add a list of numbers, you can change any number on your list and the total will change automatically. You can keep a copy of the first list and save the changes too.

Making the changes

	A	B	C
1	Item	Amount	
2	food	£12.78	
3	cinema	£5.50	
4	travel	£8.63	
5	books and CDs	£13.99	
6	drinks	£3.67	
7	newspapers	£2.35	
8	clothes	£20.00	
9	TOTAL	£66.92	

1. Make sure that the list of what you spend each week is still on your screen. Click on a cell containing an amount that has changed this week.

	A	B	C
1	Item	Amount	
2	food		
3	cinema	£5.50	
4	travel	£8.63	
5	books and CDs	£13.99	
6	drinks	£3.67	
7	newspapers	£2.35	
8	clothes	£20.00	
9	TOTAL	£54.14	

2. Press Delete so that the amount disappears. The total at the bottom of column B will change. Now type the new amount spent on that item.

	A	B	C
1	Item	Amount	
2	food	£4.20	
3	cinema	£5.50	
4	travel	£8.63	
5	books and CDs	£13.99	
6	drinks	£3.67	
7	newspapers	£2.35	
8	clothes	£20.00	
9	TOTAL	£58.34	

This is the new total.

3. Look at the total at the bottom of column B. Press Enter and watch the total change to the amount you have spent this week.

Giving another name

This section shows you how to save your new list and keep a copy of the list you made on page 26 too. You will need to find the Save As box and give your new list another name.

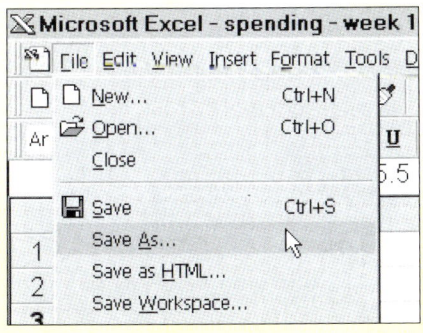

1. Move the pointer over File at the top of the screen. Click so a menu drops down. Move the pointer down the menu. When Save As is highlighted, click.

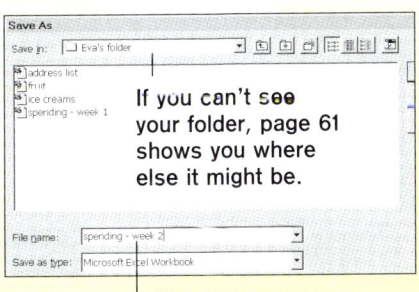

The name you type appears here.

2. The Save As box appears. Type a name, such as 'spending - week 2'. Click on Save. Now you have two spreadsheets with different names.

Item	Amount
food	£12.78
cinema	£5.50
travel	£8.63
books and CDs	£13.99
drinks	£3.67
newspapers	£2.35
clothes	£20.00
TOTAL	£66.92

Item	Amount
food	£5.00
cinema	£0.00
travel	£0.00
books and CDs	£5.99
drinks	£8.67
newspapers	£2.35
clothes	£10.00
TOTAL	£32.01

These lists show the different amounts spent for two weeks.

11. Subtracting numbers

You can type a formula to subtract one number from another. This can be useful if you want to keep track of the money you spend. If you start off by typing the total amount you have, then each time you spend something, you can subtract it from the total. This way you always know what you have left. Close the last spreadsheet you worked on, then click on the New tool.

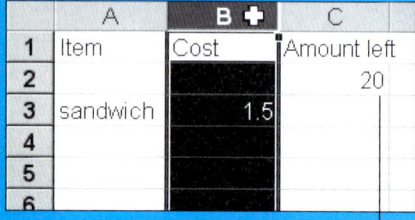

Type the total amount here.

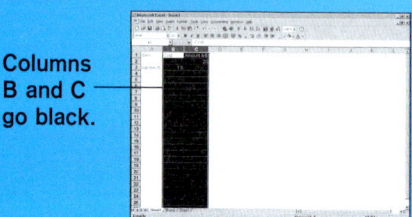

Columns B and C go black.

1. Type in all the information above. To select columns B and C, move the pointer over the box at the top of column B. Hold down the mouse button.

2. Move the pointer over the top of column C. Release the mouse button. Add currency signs to both columns using the Format Cells box.

A new formula

Here is the formula you need to subtract what you have spent from the total. It is similar to the formula you used to add numbers.

Press this key.

1. Click in cell C3. Type an equals sign, then type the coordinates of the cell where you typed the total amount, in this case cell C2.

2. To type a minus sign, press the key that has a long and a short horizontal line on (shown above). The shorter line will appear on your spreadsheet.

3. Type the coordinates of the cell that contains the amount you spent, in this case B3. Press the Enter key. The amount you have left appears.

Month	Number sold	Number left
		1000
January	120	880
February	100	780
March	240	540
April	180	360
May	140	220
June	50	170

Item	Cost	Amount left
		£20.00
sandwich	£1.50	£18.50
magazine	£2.00	£16.50
bus ticket	£1.35	£15.15
birthday card	£1.99	£13.16
chocolate bar	£0.80	£12.36

Adding more items

Each time you add another item to the list, you can repeat the formula, so you don't have to keep typing it.

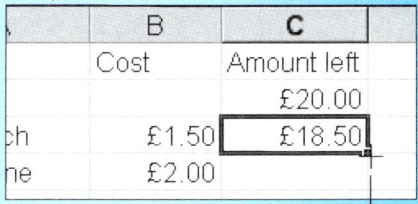

The pointer

1. Type another item in column A. Type how much it cost in column B. Click in cell C3. Move the pointer over the black square in the corner of that cell.

2. Press and hold down the mouse button as you move the pointer down over the next cell in column C. Release the mouse button.

3. The amount you have left appears in C4. Continue typing more items in columns A and B, then repeat steps 1 and 2 to subtract more numbers.

These spreadsheets use a formula to subtract one number from another.

Tip

You can follow the steps above to repeat a formula from one cell to another. You can also repeat a formula so it calculates lots of rows at once (see page 22).

12. Multiplying two numbers

Here is a Microsoft® Excel 97 formula that you can use to multiply two numbers. This example shows you how to use it to calculate how much it costs to stay in different hotels for several nights.

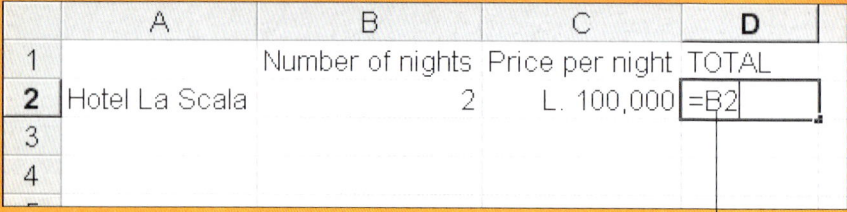
Type an equals sign and coordinates.

Press this key.

1. Use the right arrow key to move along row 1 and type in headings like the ones above. Fill in the information that you want along row 2.

2. Select columns C and D and add currency signs (see page 25). In D2, type an equals sign and the coordinates of the first cell you want to multiply.

3. To type a multiplication sign, hold down the Shift key. Press the key with a number 8 and an asterisk. The asterisk appears. Relese the Shift key.

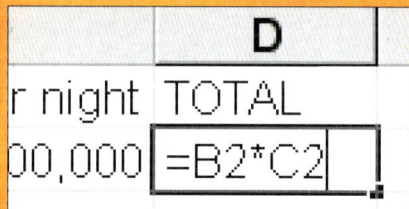

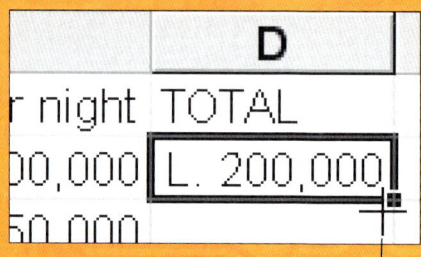
The pointer becomes thinner.

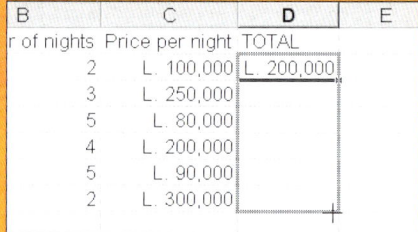

4. Type the coordinates of the second cell you want to multiply. Press the Enter key. The total will replace the formula in cell D2.

5. Fill in more of the rows in columns A, B and C. Move the pointer over the square in the corner of D2 to repeat the multiplication formula.

6. Hold down the mouse button. Move the pointer over the last cell you want to select. Release the mouse button. All the totals in the column appear.

Tour of Italy

Hotel	Number of nights	Price per night	TOTAL
Hotel La Scala, Milan	2	L. 100,000	L. 200,000
Grand Hotel, Venice	3	L. 250,000	L. 750,000
Hotel Duomo, Florence	5	L. 80,000	L. 400,000
Hotel Colosseum, Rome	4	L. 200,000	L. 800,000
Hotel Hermitage, Sorrento	5	L. 90,000	L. 450,000
Hotel Marina, Capri	2	L. 300,000	L. 600,000

13. Dividing numbers

You can divide numbers in exactly the same way that you multiply them. This time you will need to type another sign in the formula to tell your computer that you want to divide.

	A	B	C	D
1	Item	Amount	People	Amount each
2	sandwiches	150	50	=B2
3	cookies	100	50	
4	bottles of lemonade	10	50	
5	sausage rolls	200	50	
6	quiches	25	50	

Type the formula here.   Press this key.

1. Decide what you want to divide. This example shows food at a party divided by the number of people who attend. Type headings along row 1.

2. Fill in columns A, B and C. Click on D2. Type an equals sign to start the formula. Type the coordinates of the first cell you want to divide.

3. Type a divide sign, by pressing the key with a forward slash. Then type the coordinates of the cell that you want to divide by.

4. Press Enter and the total will appear. To repeat the dividing formula for each row, click on D2 and move the pointer over the square in the corner.

5. Hold down the mouse button and move the pointer down column D. When it is on the last cell you want to select, release the mouse button.

6. The total now appears for each row. If there are lots of numbers after the decimal point, page 33 shows you how to remove them.

The population per square kilometre of each country shown here is the population divided by the area.

Country	Population	Area in square kilometres	Population per square kilometre
Argentina	36,600,000	1,727,268	21
Bolivia	8,100,000	682,477	12
Brazil	168,000,000	5,309,948	32
Chile	15,000,000	470,045	32
Colombia	38,600,000	707,532	55
Ecuador	12,400,000	176,158	70
Guyana	700,000	133,547	5
Paraguay	5,200,000	252,687	21
Peru	26,600,000	798,424	33
Suriname	400,000	101,430	4
Uruguay	3,400,000	110,213	31
Venezuela	23,700,000	566,598	42

Item	Amount	People	Amount each
sandwiches	150	50	3
cookies	100	50	2
bottles of lemonade	10	50	0.2
sausage rolls	200	50	4
quiches	25	50	0.5
lemon cakes	25	50	0.5

Page 33 shows you how to remove numbers after the decimal point.

14. Finding an average

When you have a list of numbers, you may want to find the average number on the list. You can find an average using a Microsoft® Excel 97 **function**. A function is like a formula, but Excel writes the sum for you. This example shows you how to find the average age of a group of people.

Average cell

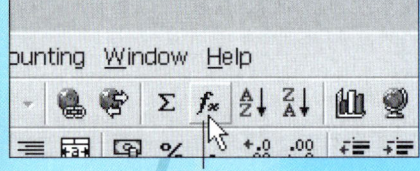
Paste Function tool

Part of the Paste Function box
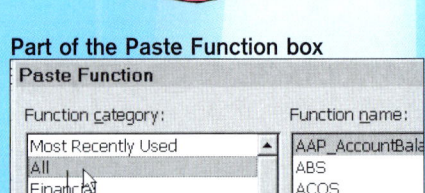
Click here.

1. Type a list of names in column A and ages in column B. Type 'AVERAGE'. Click in the cell below the list of ages. This is the average cell.

2. Find the Paste Function tool on the toolbar beside the AutoSum tool. Click on it so the Paste Function box appears on your screen.

3. The Paste Function box has two lists. On the list below Function category, on the left-hand side of the box, find the word All and click on it.

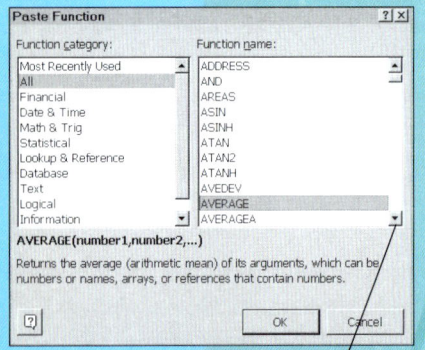
Down scroll arrow

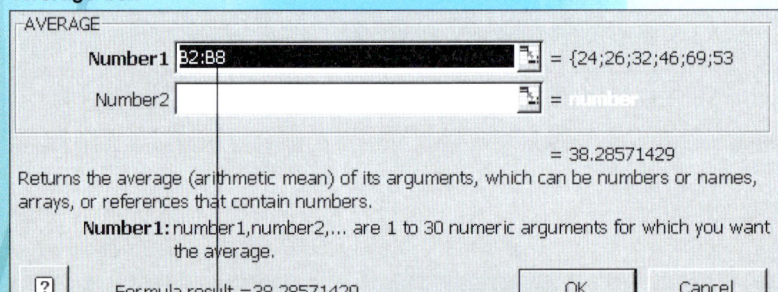
Average box

The coordinates appear here.

4. Click on the down scroll arrow beside the right-hand list, until you can see the word Average. Click on it. Click on OK. The Average box appears.

5. At the top of the box, Excel shows the coordinates of the first and the last cells in the column above the average cell. Click on OK.

6. The average age appears in the average cell. If there are lots of numbers after the decimal point, see the section on rounding up, opposite.

Here are some examples of averages.

Tip

You can also use Microsoft® Excel 97 to find the average of a row of numbers. Just click on the empty cell at the end of the row of numbers. Follow steps 2-6 above.

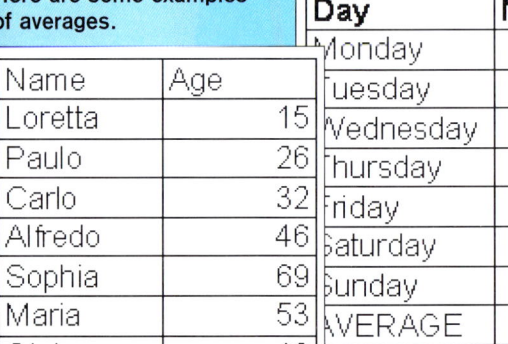

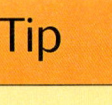

Quick averages

Here is a quick way to find averages. The average won't appear in a cell on your spreadsheet, but you will be able to see it on the strip below the horizontal scroll bar.

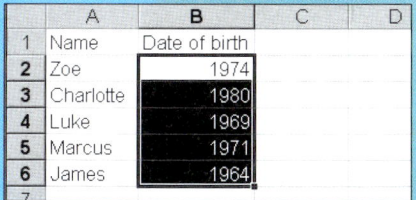 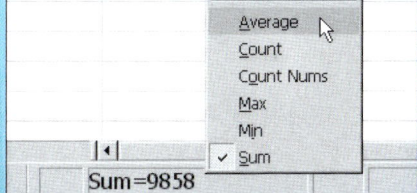 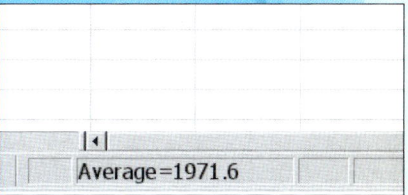

1. Select the numbers on your spreadsheet. Move the pointer over the strip below the horizontal scroll bar. Click the <u>right</u> mouse button.

2. On the menu, a tick beside Sum shows that the total, or sum of the selected numbers appears. Click the left mouse button on Average.

3. Now the average appears. To see the total again, click the right mouse button on the same strip, then click the left mouse button on Sum.

Rounding up numbers

When you find averages, or when you divide numbers, the result may have lots of numbers after the decimal point. This section shows you how to round them up to lose some of the extra decimal places.

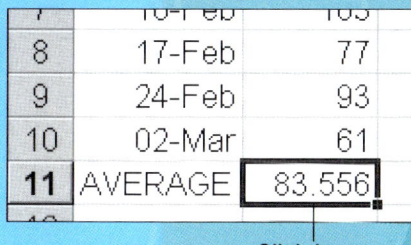 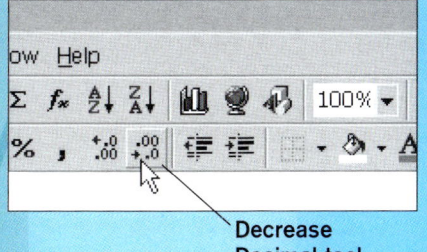

Click here.

Decrease Decimal tool

1. Click on the cell containing the average. On the toolbar, find two tools which have three zeros, two dots and a tiny arrow on (see right).

2. The right-hand tool is the Decrease Decimal tool. Each time you click on it, one number to the right of the decimal point disappears.

3. If the number that you are removing is 5 or over, the number to the left will be rounded up by one. Remove as many numbers as you need.

This example shows the average of each row on the spreadsheet (see tip on the opposite page).

	Flora's Flowers - Sales				
	June	July	August	September	Average
tulips	£100.00	£80.00	£60.00	£40.00	£70.00
lilies	£120.00	£130.00	£150.00	£140.00	£135.00
daisies	£300.00	£350.00	£320.00	£300.00	£317.50
roses	£250.00	£220.00	£230.00	£220.00	£230.00

33

15. Writing a timetable

Microsoft® Excel 97 is ideal for writing timetables, rotas or calendars. It has a shortcut you can use to speed up typing sequences of days, months, dates or times. You can make a sequence appear along a row or down a column. This page shows you how to make days appear along row 1 of a spreadsheet and times appear down column A.

Adding days

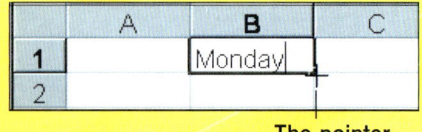
The pointer

1. Type 'Monday' in cell B1. Move the pointer over the square in the corner of B1. Hold down the mouse button and move the pointer over C1.

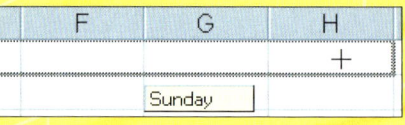

2. You will see a tiny message reading 'Tuesday'. Move the pointer until you see a message reading 'Sunday', then release the mouse button.

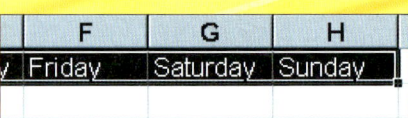

3. The days of the week from Monday to Sunday appear along row 1. You may need to widen the columns to fit in some of the words.

Typing times

The times on a timetable have to be typed in a particular way. You can change the way they look later (see the opposite page). This example is of a timetable starting at 9:00a.m.

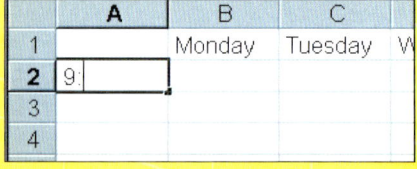

1. Click in A2 and type '9'. Type a colon sign by holding down the Shift key and pressing the key with a colon and a semi-colon on it.

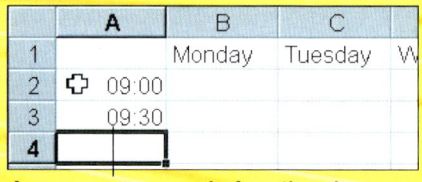
A zero may appear before the nine.

2. Press zero twice. Press Enter. To show a sequence of times that are half an hour apart, type 9:30. You can show any sequence of times you like.

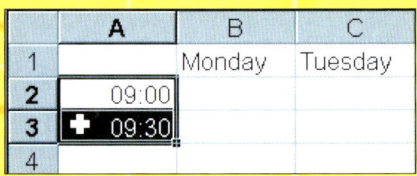

3. To continue showing times that are half an hour apart, move the pointer over A2. Hold down the mouse button as you move the pointer over A3.

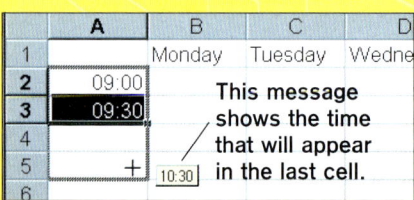
This message shows the time that will appear in the last cell.

4. Move the pointer over the square in the corner of A3. Hold down the mouse button. Move the pointer down. A message shows times that will appear.

5. When the message shows the last time that you want on the list, release the mouse button. Times half an hour apart appear. Click in any cell.

Tip

You can show sequences of dates too. Type dates in numbers, not words - you can change the style later. Press the hyphen (-) or forward slash key (/) between the month, day and year.

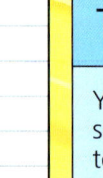

02/09/00
04/09/00
06/09/00
08/09/00
10/09/00

16. Change the way times look

There are lots of different ways you can make times look on your timetable. You can change the way dates look too. First of all, make sure your timetable from the opposite page is on your screen, then just follow the steps below.

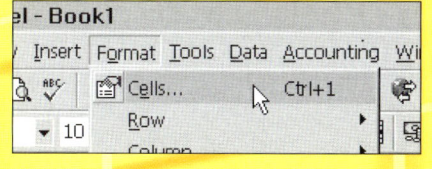

1. Click on the letter at the top of column A to select the cells containing the times that you want to change. Click on Format, then on Cells.

2. At the top of the box, click on Number. On the list below Category, click on Time to highlight it. If you typed dates, click on Date.

3. Another list appears to the right, which shows different styles of times or dates. Choose a style and click on it. Then click on OK.

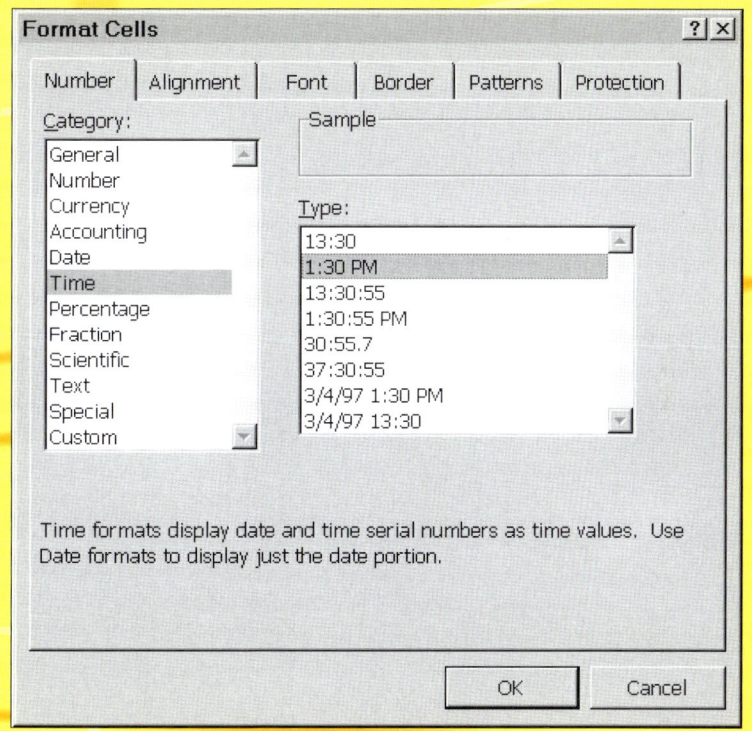

Format Cells box

Tip

Sometimes, when you change the way numbers look, symbols like these appear. This simply means the column isn't wide enough. To widen columns, double-click on the right-hand edge of the box at the top of the column.

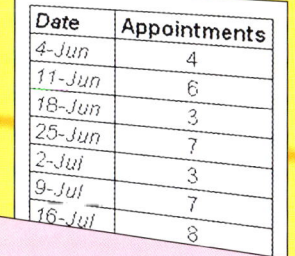

This list shows dates that are one week apart.

This timetable shows times that are one hour apart.

The rota to the right shows a sequence of days.

17. Rearranging a spreadsheet

These pages show you how to copy and move the words you've typed anywhere on your spreadsheet, without having to type them again. There are three tools that can help you. The **Copy** tool remembers what you've typed, the **Paste** tool makes a copy appear somewhere else and the **Cut** tool removes words you've typed.

Cut tool   Paste tool
Copy tool

Making copies

If you want to make a copy of any words you've typed and make them appear somewhere else, you can use the Copy and Paste tools.

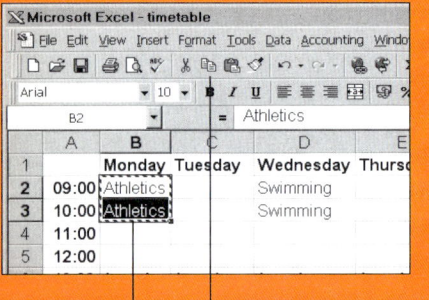

Dotted line   Copy tool

1. Select the cells that you want to copy (see page 17). Click on the Copy tool on the toolbar. A flashing, dotted line appears around the selected cells.

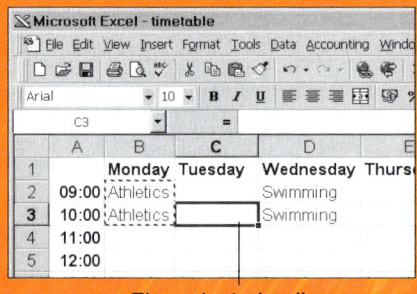

The selected cells will appear here.

2. Click on the cell at the top of the place where you want to put the copy. Remember, you can use the scroll arrows to see other parts of the screen.

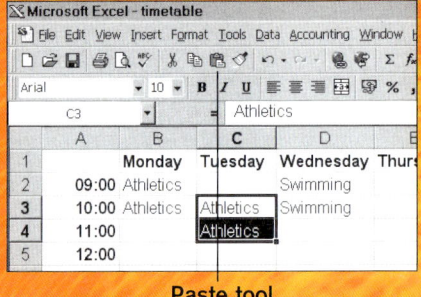

Paste tool

3. Click on the Paste tool. A copy of the cells you selected will appear in and below the cell you clicked on. Press Enter to remove the dotted lines.

Moving cells

This section shows you how to use the Cut tool to move words you've typed from one place to another on your spreadsheet.

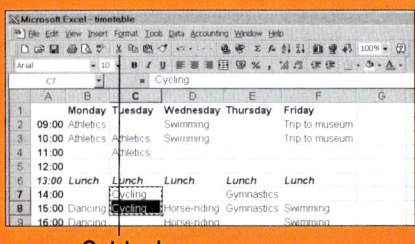

Cut tool

1. Select the cells that you want to move. Click on the Cut tool on the toolbar. A flashing, dotted line appears around the selected cells.

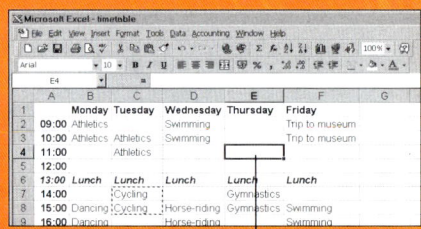

You can click in any cell.

2. Click in the cell at the top of the place where you want to move the cells to. You can use the scroll arrows to move to other parts of the screen.

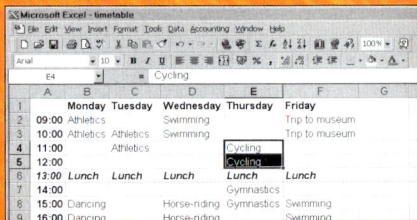

3. Click on the Paste tool. The words disappear from the place where you typed them and appear in the place you have chosen.

36

A quicker way to copy

Sometimes it is easier to use the keyboard than the mouse to give your computer instructions. These steps show you a quick way to copy cells using the keyboard. You can move cells this way too.

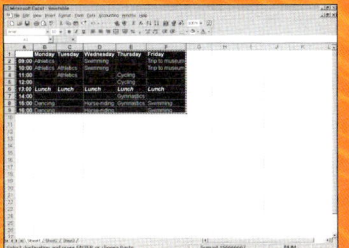 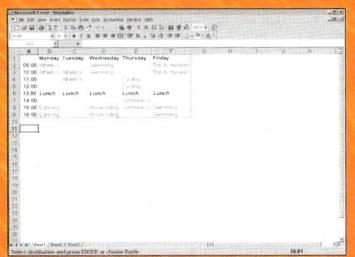 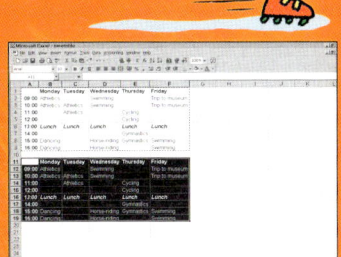

1. Select the cells you want to copy. Instead of clicking on the Copy tool, hold down the Ctrl key. Press the letter C. Then, release the Ctrl key.

2. You will see a flashing, dotted line around the selected cells. Click in the cell at the top of the place where you want the copy to appear.

3. To paste the selected cells where you clicked, hold down the Ctrl key while you press the letter V. Press Enter to remove the dotted line.

A quicker way to move cells

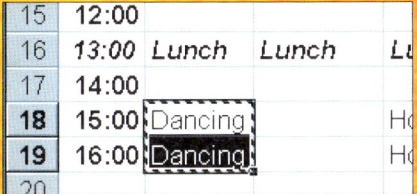

1. First select the cells you want to move. Instead of clicking on the Cut tool, hold down the Ctrl key while you press the letter X.

2. A dotted line appears around the cells you selected. Click on the cell at the top of the place where you want the selected cells to appear.

3. Hold down the Ctrl key while you press the letter V. The selected cells move to the place where you clicked. Remember to save the changes.

This example shows the same timetable copied three times.

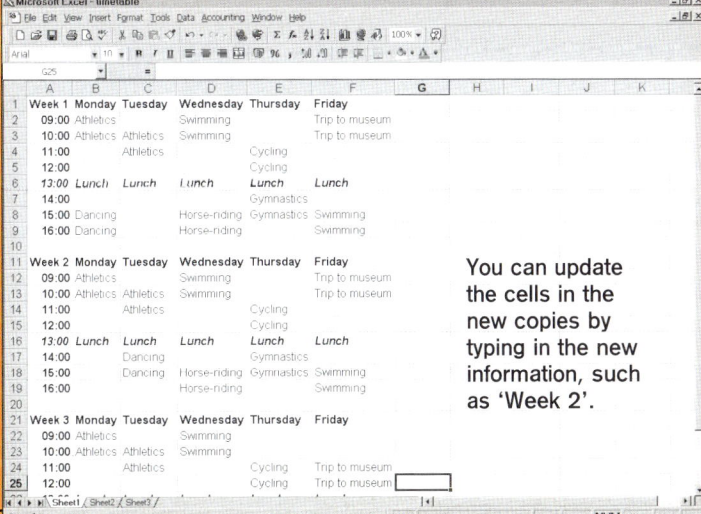

You can update the cells in the new copies by typing in the new information, such as 'Week 2'.

Tip

You can speed things up even more. After you have cut or copied the selected cells, click on the cell where you want to paste them. Then, just press the Enter key.

You can find out about more keyboard shortcuts on page 62.

18. Fitting in more

When you type a lot of words in a cell, you have probably noticed that they appear in a long line. This can be a nuisance if you want to type long sentences, such as detailed plans on a calendar. These pages show you how to change the width and the height of cells so you can fit in as many words as you like.

Making a calendar

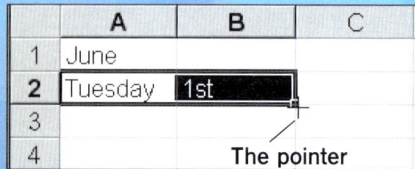
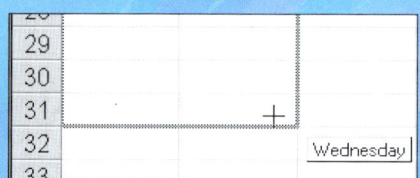

1. Type the month in A1. Type the first day of the month in A2 and '1st' in B2. Select A2 and B2. Move the pointer over the square in the corner of B2.

2. Hold down the mouse button. Move the pointer down column B. When a message shows the last day, release. Type your plans in column C. Press Enter.

Here is an example of a spreadsheet with several lines of typing in one cell.

Choosing the column width

You found out how to widen columns to fit in all your words on page 12. These steps show you how to choose the column width. If words still spill into the next column, you can move them onto more lines (see opposite).

1. Move the pointer over the right-hand edge of the box at the top of column C. The pointer will change to a double arrow shape.

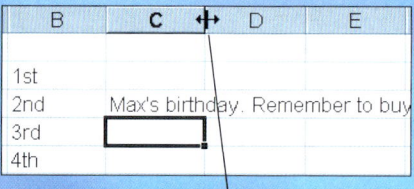
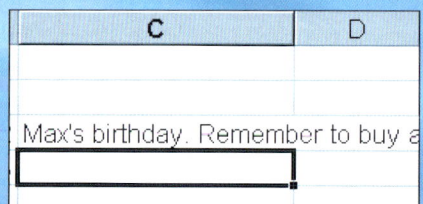

2. Hold down the mouse button and move the pointer to the right. A dotted line shows you that the edge of the column is moving too.

3. Position the edge of the column where you want it to go and release the mouse button. See the opposite page to move any extra words.

June		
Tuesday	1st	
Wednesday	2nd	Max's birthday. Remember to buy a gift.
Thursday	3rd	
Friday	4th	
Saturday	5th	Visit Grandpa. Remember to take photos.
Sunday	6th	
Monday	7th	
Tuesday	8th	
Wednesday	9th	Return library books.
Thursday	10th	
Friday	11th	
Saturday	12th	Sponsored walk. Meet by town hall.
Sunday	13th	
Monday	14th	
Tuesday	15th	
Wednesday	16th	
Thursday	17th	Go to see with Ben.
Friday	18th	
Saturday	19th	
Sunday	20th	
Monday	21st	
Tuesday	22nd	

ITEM
BUCKETS
SPADES
SUNGLASSES

Adding more lines

This section shows you how to change the height of a cell, so you can fit more lines of words into it.

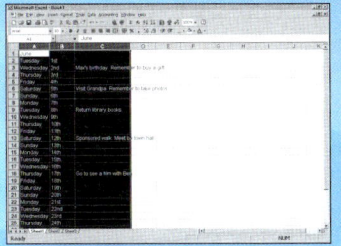

Columns A, B and C are selected.

1. Move the pointer over the top of column A. Hold down the mouse button and move the pointer over the top of column C, then release.

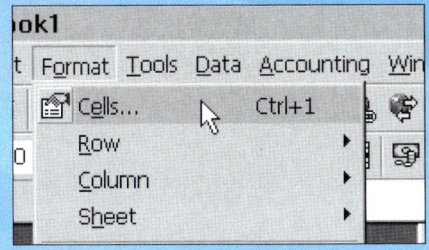

2. Click on Format, then click on Cells on the menu. The Format Cells box appears. At the top of the box, click on the word Alignment (see below).

Part of the Format Cells box

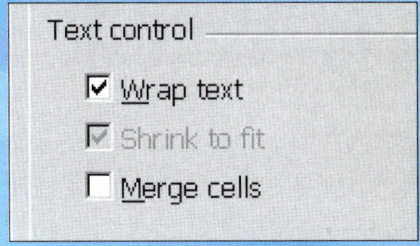

3. To move the words in a cell onto more than one line, click on the box beside Wrap text, in the Text control section, so a tick appears.

4. Click on the box below the word Vertical. On the menu that drops down, click on Top. This makes your typing start at the top of each cell.

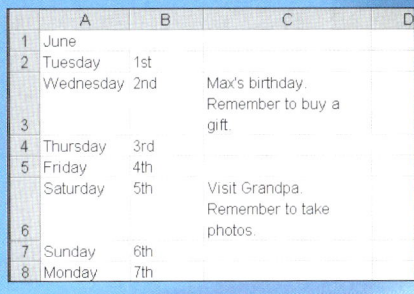

Format Cells box

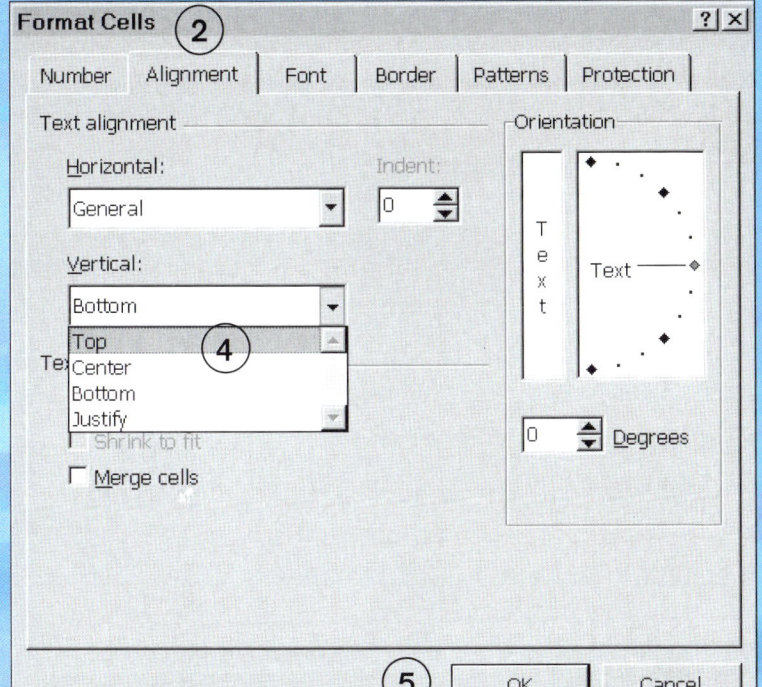

5. Click on OK, so that the Format Cells box disappears. Any words that spilled into the next column now move onto another line.

If your spreadsheet has long headings, you can make the headings appear on several lines.

19. Sorting lists

When you type long lists, it isn't always easy to find the information you want. The example on this page shows you how to sort a simple index into alphabetical or numerical order so you can find what you're looking for more easily. You can sort lists of books, documents or CDs this way too.

Alphabetical order

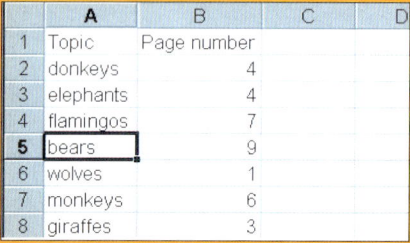 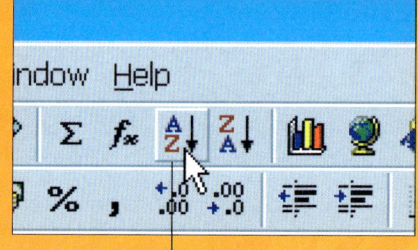

Sort Ascending tool

1. Type the headings, shown above, along row 1. Then, fill in the information you want in columns A and B. Click in any cell in column A.

2. To put column A into alphabetical order with A at the top and Z at the bottom, click on the Sort Ascending tool on the toolbar.

3. The words in column A move into alphabetical order. The numbers move too. If your headings move, follow steps 2-3 opposite, then press Enter.

Numerical order

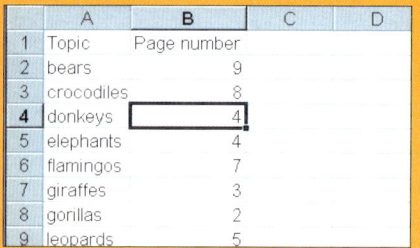 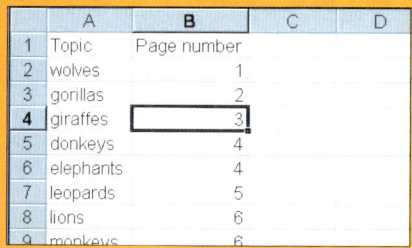

1. If you prefer, you can put the numbers in column B into numerical order. Click on any cell in column B, then click on the Sort Ascending tool.

2. The numbers move into numerical order with the lowest number at the top and the highest at the bottom. The words in column A move too.

Tip

Sort Descending tool

If you want to sort a list of words so Z is at the top and A is at the bottom, or if you want to sort a list of numbers so the highest number is at the top, just click on the Sort Descending tool. The Sort Descending tool is to the right of the Sort Ascending tool on the toolbar.

The spreadsheet on the right has three columns. The dates are in ascending numerical order – the earliest date is at the top.

Artist	Album	Year
The Beatles	Hard Day's Night	1964
Rolling Stones	Beggars Banquet	1968
The Clash	The Clash	1977
Abba	Super Trouper	1978
Spandau Ballet	Singles Collection	1985
Nirvana	Unplugged	1992
Spice Girls	Spiceworld	1997
Madonna	Ray of Light	1998

Sorting more columns

These steps show you how to sort an address list by putting the countries into alphabetical order and the surnames of the people in each country into alphabetical order too.

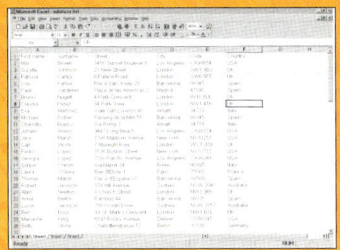

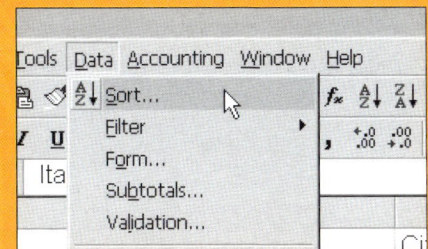

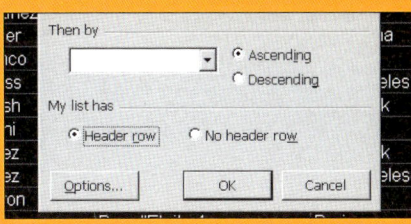

Part of the Sort box

1. Open your address list from pages 12-13. If you've forgotten how to reopen a spreadsheet that you've saved, turn to page 57.

2. Click on the word Data at the top of the screen. On the menu that drops down, click on Sort. The Sort box will appear on your screen.

3. Near the bottom of the Sort box, you will see the words Header row. Click on the white dot beside Header row so a black dot appears.

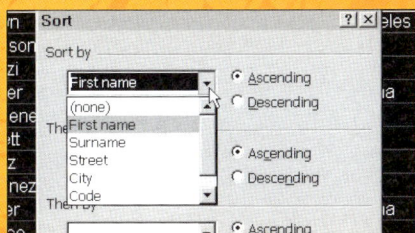

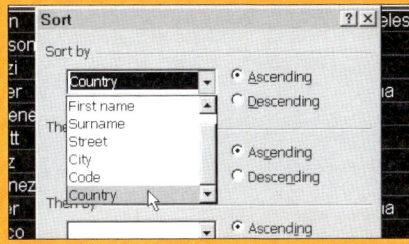

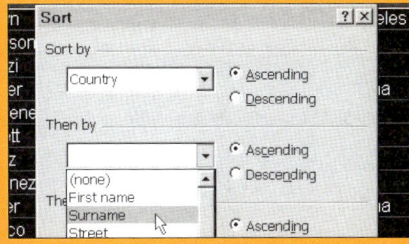

4. In the 'Sort by' section, you'll see a box with a down arrow beside it. Click on the arrow so a menu appears showing your column headings.

5. Find Country and click on it. You may need to click on the arrow at the bottom of the menu. Click on the dot beside Ascending, in the same section.

6. In the 'Then by' section, click on the down arrow beside the white box. Another menu appears showing your column headings. Click on Surname.

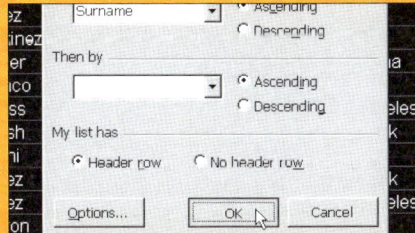

7. Click so there is a black dot beside Ascending in the same section. Click on OK. Click to remove the black background, then save the changes.

The countries on the address list below are in alphabetical order. The surnames of the people in each country are in alphabetical order too.

First Name	Surname	Street	City	Code	Country
Lucia	Jackson	156 Ocean Drive	Sydney	NSW 2057	Australia
Robert	Jackson	879 Hill Avenue	Sydney	NSW 2048	Australia
Laura	O'Shea	Rue d'Etoile	Paris	75003	France
Charlotte	Bianco	Via Roma 3	Amalfi	84789	Italy
Sophie	Chiron	Via Napoli 34	Rome	00197	Italy
Eva	Martinez	Viale San Lorenzo 46	Amalfi	84739	Italy
Anna	Bellini	Ramblas 44	Barcelona	08026	Spain
Michael	Fisher	Passeig de la Mer 55	Barcelona	08345	Spain
Paulo	Gardener	Plaza de las Americas 2	Madrid	47890	Spain
Thomas	Marsh	Placa d'Espana 87	Barcelona	08509	Spain
Lola	Parker	Placa San Josep 28	Barcelona	08354	Spain
Patrizia	Carlizi	6 Palace Road	London	SW6 5FE	UK
Suzette	Johnson	23 New Street	London	SW1 9BJ	UK
Alain	Newton	8 Church Street	London	NW3 9RK	UK
Bruno	Nugett	4 Park Crescent	London	W11 8UK	UK
Hemali	Singh	7 Castle View	Knaresborough	HG5 8TB	UK
Max	Brown	3456 Sunset Boulevard	Los Angeles	CA98654	USA

20. Finding information

When you need to find particular information from a long list, it helps if you can narrow down the choices. In computer jargon, this is called filtering. These pages show you how to filter a list of soccer results so that only the information about a particular player appears. You can try filtering other kinds of lists too.

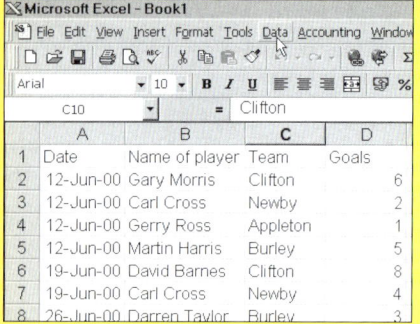

1. Type a list of results, like the one above. Click on any cell that you have typed in. Find the word Data at the top of the screen and click on it.

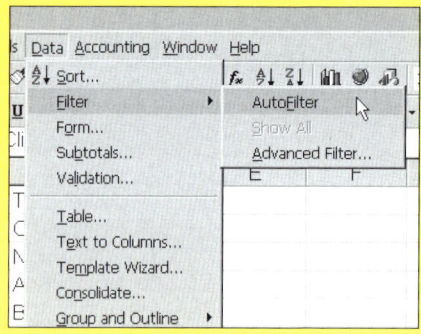

2. On the menu that drops down, click on Filter. On the next menu, click on AutoFilter. A tiny arrow will appear at the top of each column.

3. To see only the information about one player, click on the arrow at the top of the player column. A list appears showing all the players on the list.

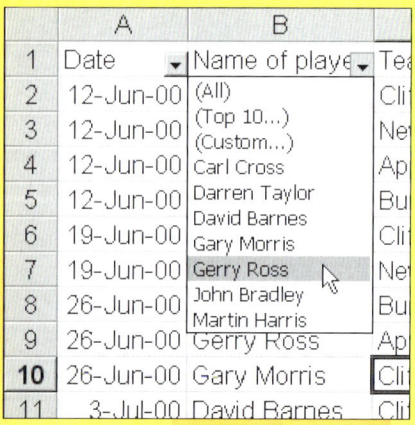

4. Choose the player you want from the list and click on the name. All the information on your list disappears except the information about that player.

See all the rows

The information about the other players on your list hasn't disappeared forever! Follow these steps to find it again.

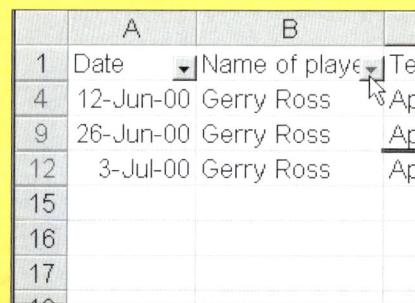

1. The arrow at the top of the column you filtered becomes blue. Click on the blue arrow so a list drops down.

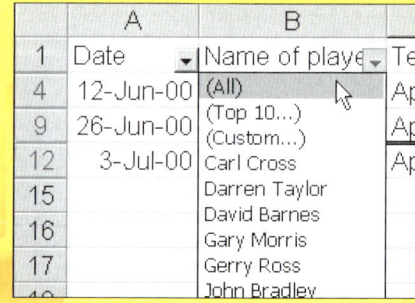

2. Click on (All) to see all the players on your list again. Click on Data, Filter, then AutoFilter to remove the arrows.

More choices

There are all sorts of choices you can make when you filter lists. This is especially useful if you want to filter numbers. The example on this page shows you how to filter a survey so you can analyze the interests of people of different ages.

1. Type headings along row 1 including Name, Age and Interests. You can add other headings if you like. Then, fill in the columns.

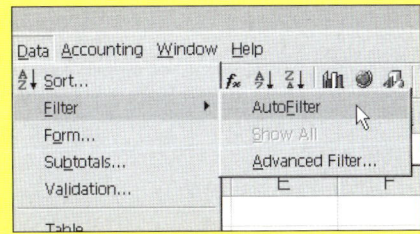

2. Click on any cell you have typed in. Click on Data, then on Filter, then on AutoFilter. Tiny arrows will appear at the top of each column.

3. Click on the arrow at the top of the column containing ages. On the list, click on (Custom...). A Custom AutoFilter box appears on your screen.

Custom AutoFilter box

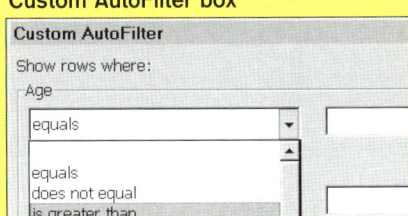

4. Click on the white box below the word Age. A list of options drops down. Choose an option, such as 'is greater than' and click on it.

Insertion point

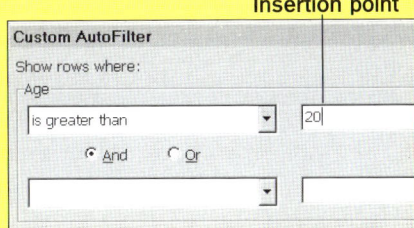

5. Click on the white box to the right, so that an insertion point appears. If you type '20', your list will only show the details of people older than 20.

6. Click on OK. The Custom AutoFilter box disappears. All the rows on your list disappear except the ones with details of people who are over 20.

Click here.

This spreadsheet shows the interests of people who have lived in this town for 20 years or more.

Name	Age	Interests	Years in town
Anna	86	painting	86
Tim	22	pop	22
Emma	92	golf	56
Cassandra	40	painting	40
Sam	26	football	20
Chris	52	football	50

Name	Age	Interests	Years in town
Clare	13	reading	11
Becky	8	ballet	8
Ben	6	playing	6
Peter	16	swimming	16

This spreadsheet shows the interests of people who are aged 18 or under.

Tip

The Custom AutoFilter box contains lots of other ways of filtering, such as finding words that begin or end with certain letters of the alphabet.

21. Using the Chart Wizard

Up to now, you have found out how to organize and calculate all sorts of information, but your spreadsheets still look like long lists. These pages show you how to make them more eye-catching using a Wizard. In computer language, a Wizard is a series of boxes that helps you make choices. These pages show you how to use the **Chart Wizard** to make a pie chart, but there are lots of other charts you can choose from, too.

Making a pie chart

Pie charts display each number on a list as one section of a circle, or pie. Before you start, make sure you have one column of numbers on your screen.

Choosing a chart

You will find some charts better than others for displaying certain kinds of information. For example, a pie chart is a good way to display one column of numbers. If you want to compare more columns or rows, a column chart is best. Line graphs are a good way to show how something changes over time. See pages 46-47 to find out about other charts.

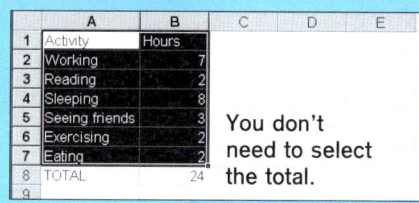

You don't need to select the total.

1. Select the cells that contain the information you want to display. Include the headings, but not a total, an average or any empty cells.

Chart Wizard tool

2. Click on the Chart Wizard tool on the toolbar. The first Chart Wizard box appears (see left). At the top of the box, click on Standard Types.

This is the first of four Chart Wizard boxes.

When you click on Standard Types, it looks as though it is in front of Custom Types.

This list shows some of the charts and graphs you can choose from.

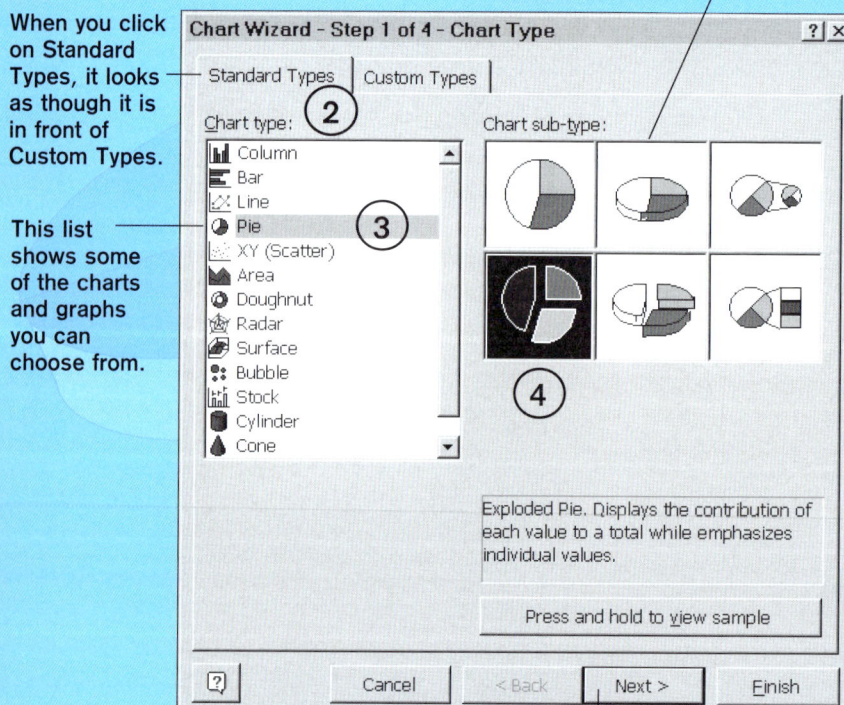

Click on one of these chart designs.

Click on Next to see the next Chart Wizard box.

3. On the left-hand side of the box, you will see a list of charts. Click on Pie so that a choice of pie chart designs appears in the box.

4. Choose one of the four left-hand pie chart designs. Click on it to select it. To see the next Chart Wizard box, click on Next, at the bottom of this box.

5. The second Chart Wizard box should look like the one to the right. If it doesn't, click on the words Data Range near the top of the box.

6. The numbers on your spreadsheet are in a column, so there should be a black dot beside Columns. If there isn't, click so that a dot appears.

Make sure there is a black dot beside Columns.

Click here.

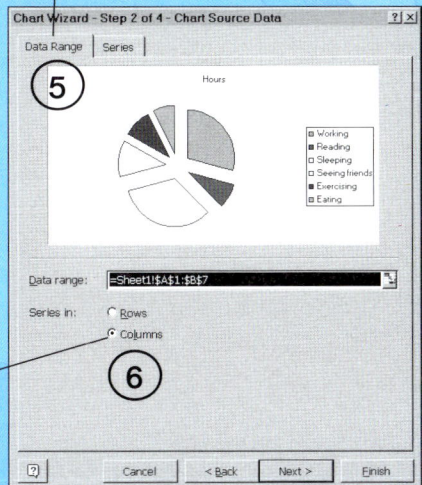

Here are some of the other pie chart designs you can choose from the first Chart Wizard box.

Type a title for your chart here.

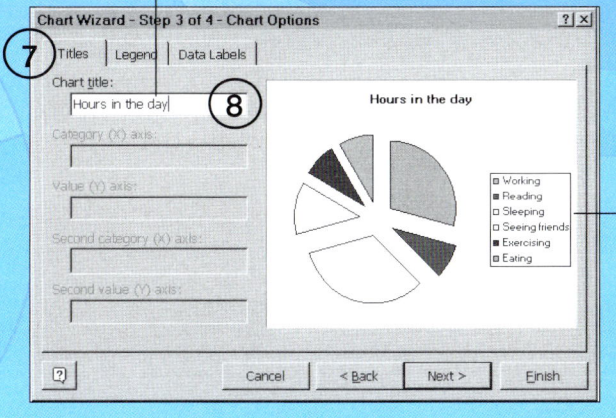

This box is called the legend. It shows what each section of the chart represents.

7. Click on Next so that a third box appears (see left). Above the chart, you'll see a title. If you want to change it, click on Titles at the top of the box.

8. Click in the Chart title box, then type a title. To add labels or percentages beside each section of the chart, click on Data Labels for more options.

Part of the last Chart Wizard box

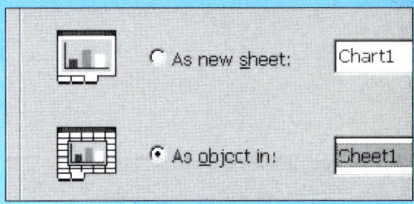

9. When you are happy with your chart, click on Next. To make the chart appear on this spreadsheet, not on a new one, choose 'As object in'.

10. Click on Finish. The chart appears on your screen (see left). Click on any cell. If you want to print your chart, there is a tip to help you on page 52.

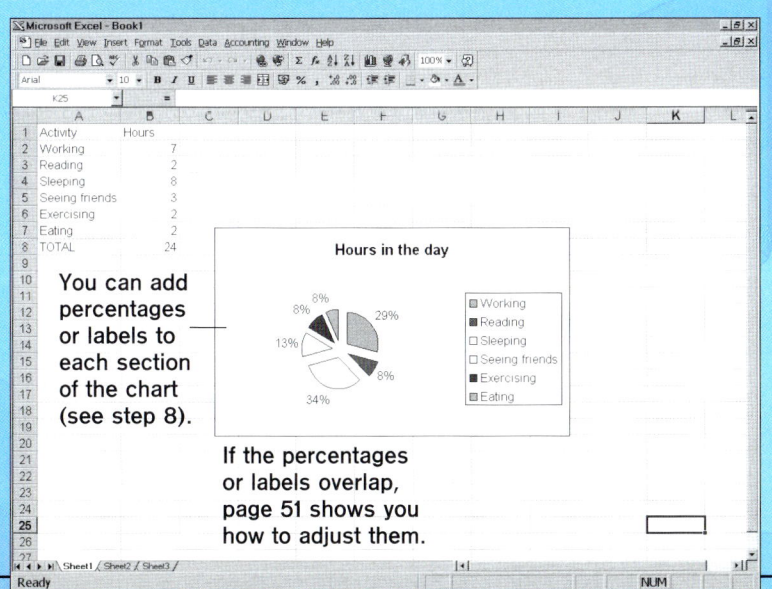

You can add percentages or labels to each section of the chart (see step 8).

If the percentages or labels overlap, page 51 shows you how to adjust them.

45

22. Making a column chart

You can make lots of other charts in the same way as a pie chart, but for each one, you need to make slightly different choices. These pages show you how to make a column chart (similar to a bar graph) to display high jump results. Column charts are especially useful if you want to compare several rows or columns of numbers, but you can display any information you want.

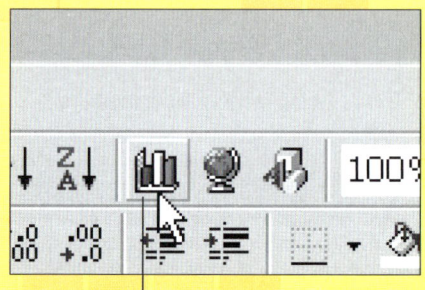

Chart Wizard tool

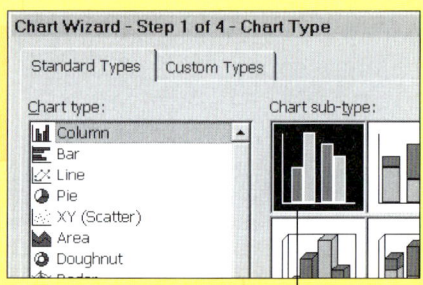

Click here.

1. Type names down column A. Type months along row 1. Fill in the results, in this case, height. Select all the cells you've typed in.

2. Click on the Chart Wizard tool on the toolbar. The first Chart Wizard box will appear. At the top of the box, click on Standard Types.

3. Below Chart type, click on Column. A choice of column charts appears. Click on the chart in the top left-hand corner. Then, click on Next.

Click so Data Range appears to be in front of Series.

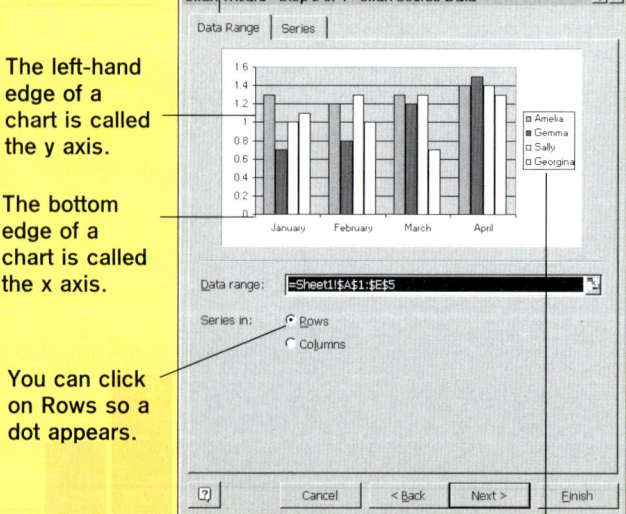

The left-hand edge of a chart is called the y axis.

The bottom edge of a chart is called the x axis.

You can click on Rows so a dot appears.

The names you typed in column A appear in the legend.

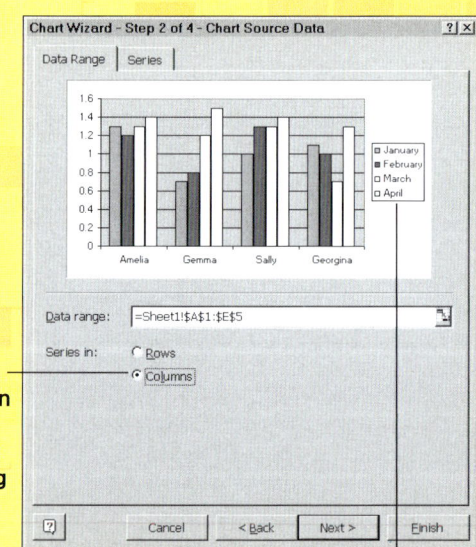

Click on Columns, to make column A from your spreadsheet appear along the x axis.

When you click on Columns, the months from row 1 appear in the legend.

4. Click on Data Range. You will see a dot beside Rows. The headings from row 1 of your spreadsheet appear along the bottom of the chart (the x axis).

5. You can now choose to switch the chart around and display the columns from your spreadsheet instead. Just click on the dot beside Columns.

6. The names you typed down column A now appear along the x axis. In this example, the results are clearer than if the months were along the x axis.

7. Click on Next, then on Titles. Click on the top white box and type a chart title. In the next two boxes down type titles for the x axis and the y axis.

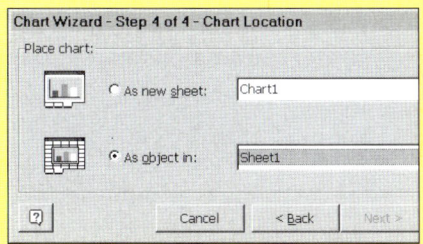

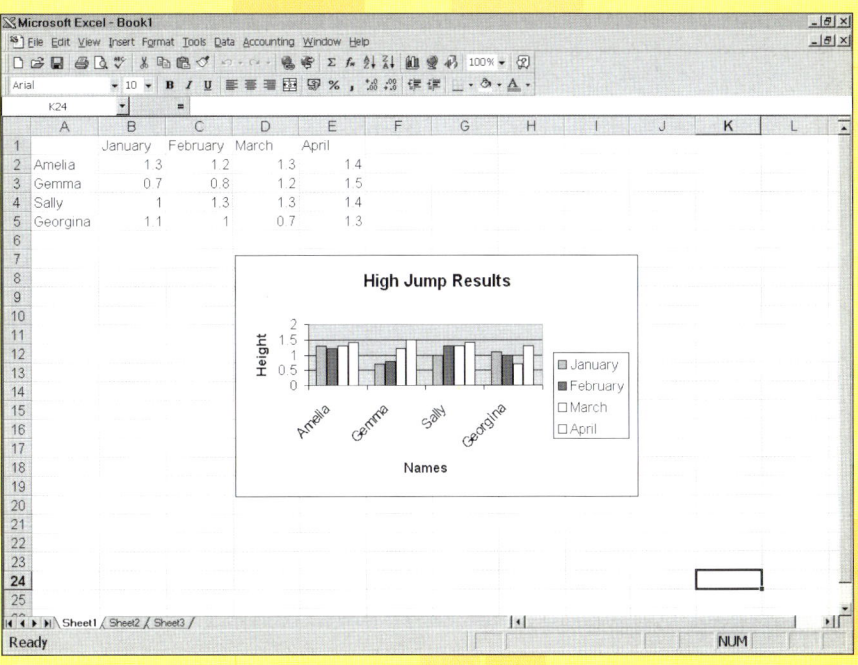

8. Click on Next. Then, click on the dot beside As object in. Click on Finish to make your chart appear on the screen, then click on any cell.

More charts

If you want to try some of the other charts from the list on the first Chart Wizard box, you can check what they will look like before you create them. Just click on the label that reads 'Press and hold to view sample' to see a preview and a description of the chart you choose.

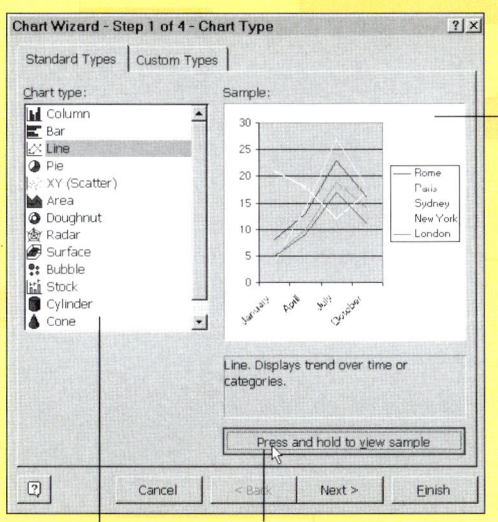

Click on some of the other charts from this list.

Click here and hold down the mouse button.

A preview appears here. This line graph shows temperatures at different times of the year.

This cone chart makes it difficult to understand this information.

These charts show the same results as the line graph to the left.

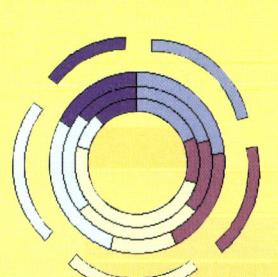

This is a doughnut chart. Again it is difficult to interpret this information.

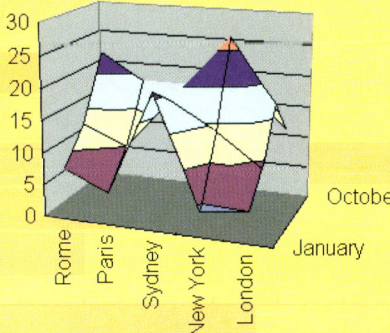

This surface graph, above, would be more useful for displaying other kinds of information.

47

23. Making words stand out

Microsoft® Excel 97 has lots of tools you can use to change the way lettering looks. This page shows you how you can use some of these tools to make certain words on your spreadsheet stand out.

Bold, italic and underlined lettering

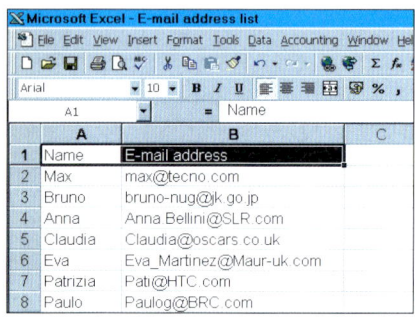

1. First of all, you will need to select the cells containing the words that you want to change. You can select any part of a spreadsheet to change.

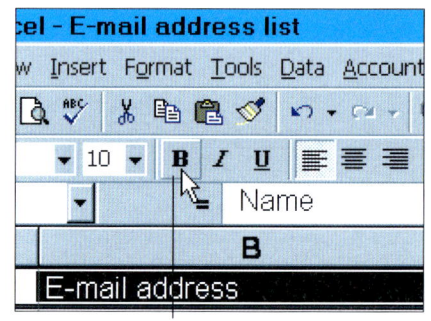

Bold tool

2. To make the lettering look thicker, move the pointer over the Bold tool. This is a capital letter B near the top of the screen. Click on it.

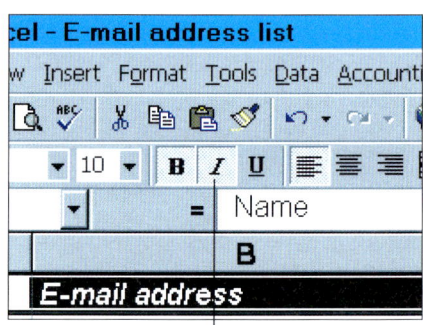

Italic tool

3. Next to the Bold tool, you will find a capital letter I. This is called the Italic tool. Click on the Italic tool to make all the lettering lean to the right.

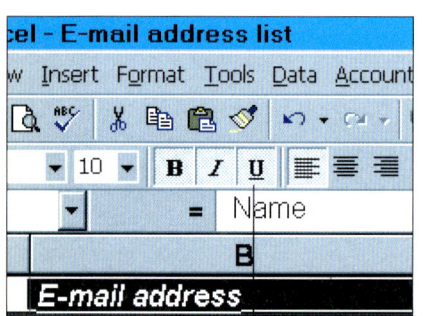

Underline tool

4. To underline the lettering, click on the capital letter U, which is on the toolbar beside the Italic tool. This is called the Underline tool.

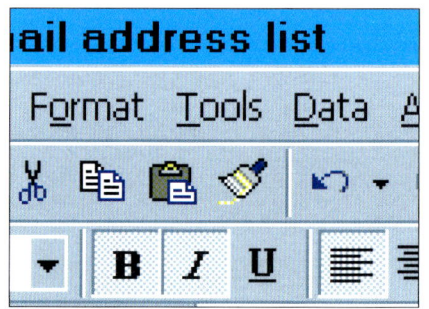

The Bold and Italic tools are switched on.

5. All these three tools work like on/off switches. When you switch one on, it looks like a pressed-in button. To switch it off, click on it again.

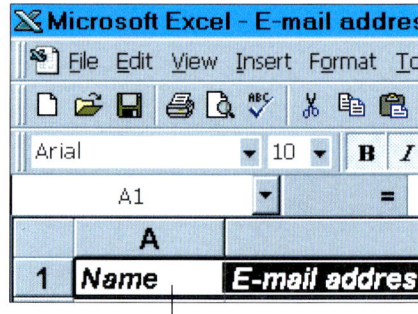

This lettering is bold and italic.

6. Click to remove the black background. If the new style takes up too much space, you will need to widen the columns (see page 12 or page 38).

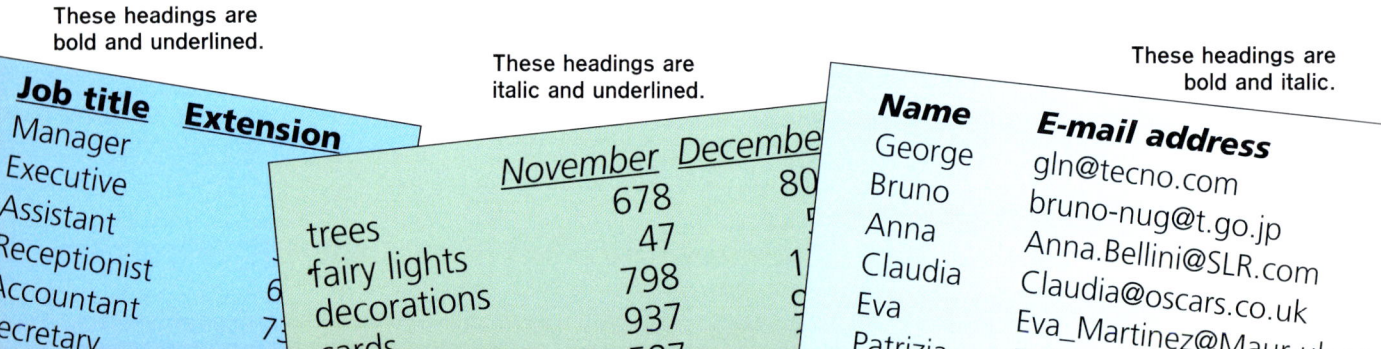

24. Different lettering styles

This page shows you how to change the style and size of the letters you type. There are lots of letter styles you can use, called **fonts**. Some look professional, while others are more unusual – you can have fun choosing which to use. Your computer may have different fonts from the ones shown here.

These are the names of some fonts you may find on your computer.

AvantGarde
Benguiat
Boulevard
Concorde
Courier

Bike DT
Friz Quadrata
Giddyup
Univers Black
Eras Demi

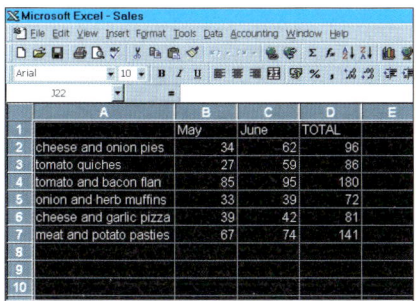

1. You can either select just a few cells, or you can select all the letters on the spreadsheet. To select them all, hold down the Ctrl key and press A.

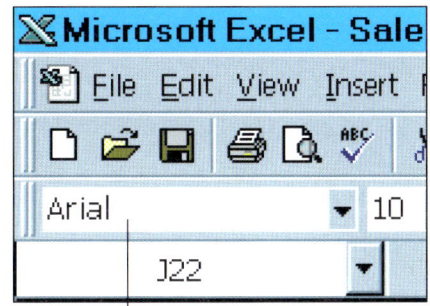

This is the Font box.

2. Below the Save tool, you will find a word written inside a white box. The word is the name of the font you've been using, in this case Arial.

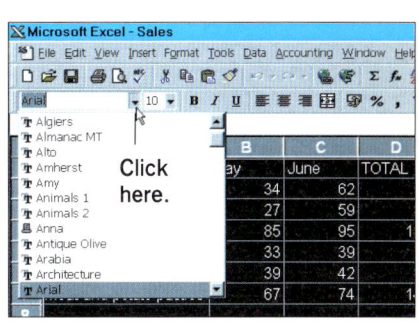

3. Move the pointer over the small arrow beside the Font box and click on it. A menu drops down, displaying the names of other fonts.

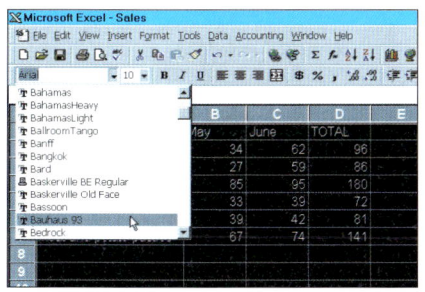

4. To see more fonts, click on the arrows beside the list. Move the pointer over a font name and click. All the letters change to the new font.

This font is called Bike DT. The headings are bold and underlined.

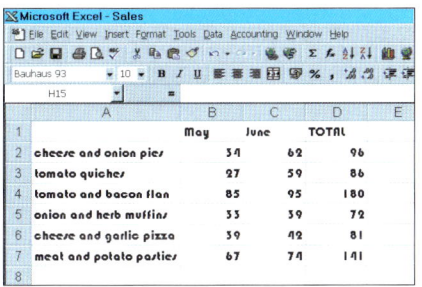

You may need to widen some columns.

5. Click on any cell to make the screen white again. To try another font, hold down Ctrl and press A, then choose another font from the Font box.

This font is called Calisto MT. The headings are size 14 and bold.

Letter size

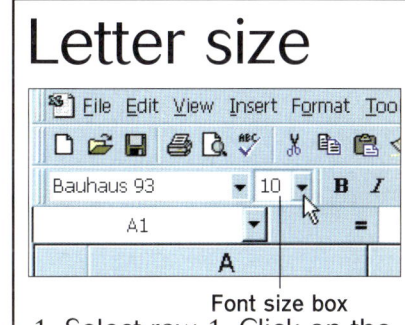

Font size box

1. Select row 1. Click on the arrow beside the white box that contains a number. This number is the font size.

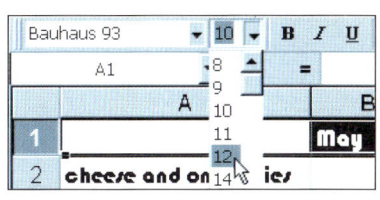

2. A list of more font sizes appears. Click on 12 to make the letters slightly bigger. Click on a higher number to make them even bigger.

25. Adding borders

Spreadsheets can look much neater if you add borders, or lines, around some of the cells. This page shows you how to add borders around all the cells you've typed in, or around just one or two.

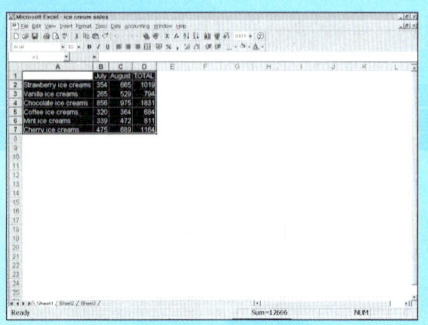

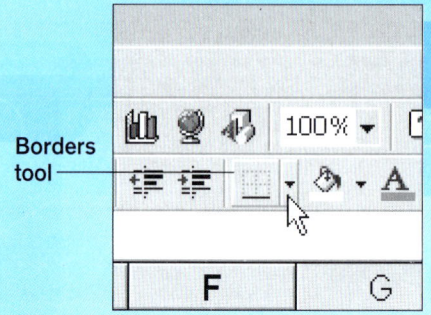

Borders tool

1. Select the cells that you want to add borders to. Only select part of the spreadsheet or you may have problems later (see the tip opposite).

2. On the toolbar, find the Borders tool. It has four little squares on. Click on the down arrow beside it. A box appears showing groups of squares.

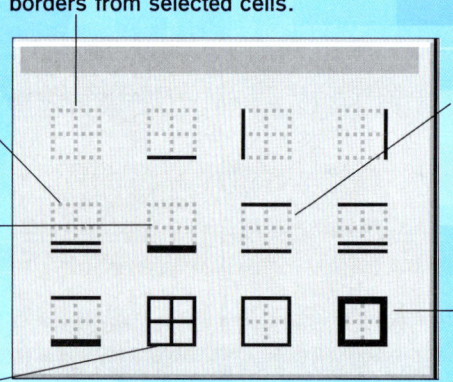

Click here to add a double line to the bottom edge of cells.

Click here to add a thick line to the bottom edge of cells.

Click here to add lines around all the cells you've selected.

Click here to remove all the borders from selected cells.

Squares with a line along the top and bottom, like this, add a line to the top and bottom of the selected cells.

Click on this to add a thick border to the outside edge of cells.

3. The groups of squares represent the cells on your spreadsheet. The bold lines represent borders. Try some out by clicking on them.

4. If you want to remove all the borders from an area of your spreadsheet, you can click on the squares that have no bold lines around them.

	APRIL	MAY	JUNE	AVERAGE
LOUISA	50	50	50	50
MARCO	100	87	93	93
RAJESH	40	45	50	45
CARLA	50	35	40	42
THERESA	50	40	100	63
MIKE	60	70	100	77
TOTAL	350	327	433	370

Hours of sunshine

April	6
May	7
June	
July	
August	
September	

	Monda
dance	Shena
gym	Carla
aerobics	Melanie
swimming	Laura

26. Bright backgrounds

Bright backgrounds can make any spreadsheet look more interesting. Have some fun experimenting with different combinations of backgrounds and borders. See pages 18-19 to find out how to print backgrounds. If your printer can't print in colour, the backgrounds will appear as different shades of grey.

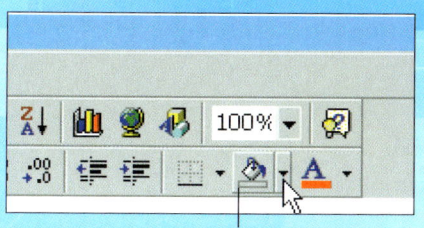

Fill Color tool

1. Select the cells you want to change. Find the Fill Color tool on the toolbar. It looks a little like a paint pot. Click on the down arrow to its right.

2. A box drops down showing lots of different colours. Choose the colour you want and click on it. Then click in an empty cell.

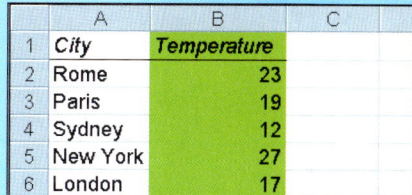

3. The cells you selected now appear in the colour you chose. Try out some more colours. Remember to save the changes you have made.

Removing backgrounds

If you decide you don't want the backgrounds you chose anymore, you can easily remove them.

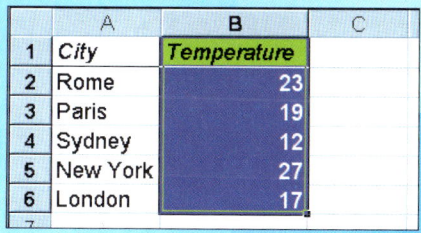

1. Select the cells that contain backgrounds you want to remove. All the cells except the first one change colour.

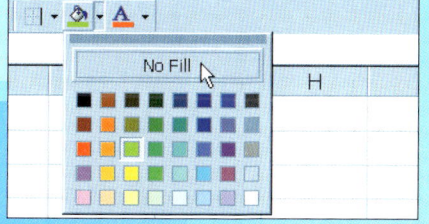

2. Click on the down arrow to the right of the Fill Color tool. Click on the words No Fill at the top of the box.

Tip

When you add backgrounds or borders, always select cells by clicking on the cells themselves. If you click on the column letter or row number, then print your work onto paper (see pages 18-19), the whole column or row prints. Each column and row contains hundreds of cells and will print on lots of pieces of paper.

Here are some spreadsheets with different borders and backgrounds.

27. Changing charts

Once you have made a chart, you can move it around your spreadsheet, change its size and experiment with different styles of lettering and backgrounds. First of all, reopen a spreadsheet where you have made a chart (see page 57).

Moving a chart

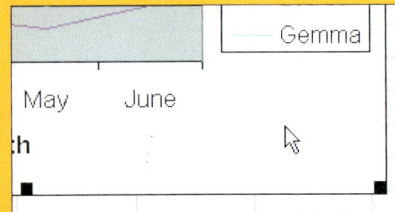 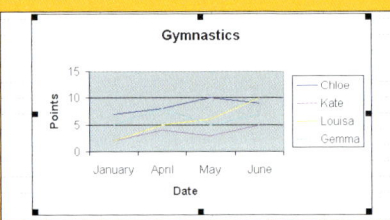 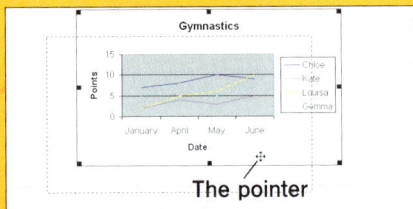

1. You will need to select the box containing the chart. To do this, move the pointer over the area near the edge of the box, then click.

2. Eight black squares around the edge of the box show that the box is selected. Hold down the mouse button and move the pointer.

3. As the pointer moves, an outline of the box moves too. When the outline is over the place where you want the chart to be, release the button.

Different sizes

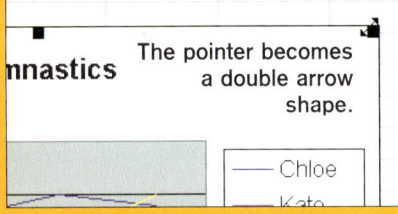 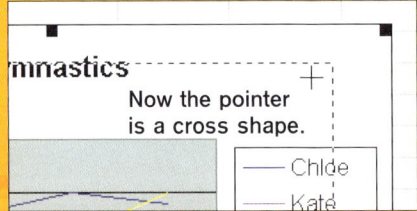

1. To change the size of the chart box, select it (see step 1 above). Move the pointer over the square in the top right-hand corner of the box.

2. Hold down the mouse button and move the pointer until a dotted line shows the size of box you want. Then release the mouse button.

Tips

1. You can update information displayed on your chart. Just click on the cell that you want to change and type in the new information. Press Enter and watch the chart update.

2. To print a chart so it fills a whole piece of paper, select the chart, then print. If you want to see the information you typed on your spreadsheet too, click on any cell before you print.

Here are some of the effects that you will find out how to create on the opposite page. The chart below has a white marble texture.

This chart has a yellow and orange gradient background and an orange border.

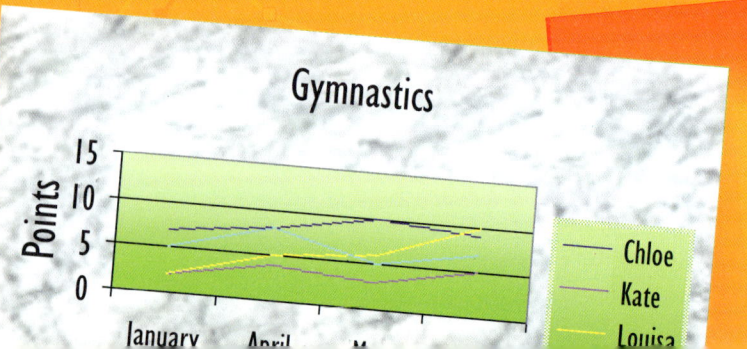
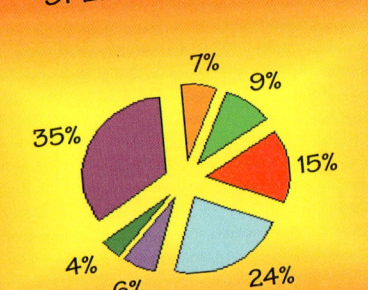

Changing styles

These steps show you how to change the style of lettering and the background of your chart.

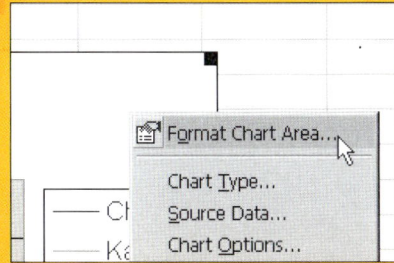

1. Move the pointer near the edge of the chart box. Press the right mouse button. Click on Format Chart Area on the menu. A box will appear.

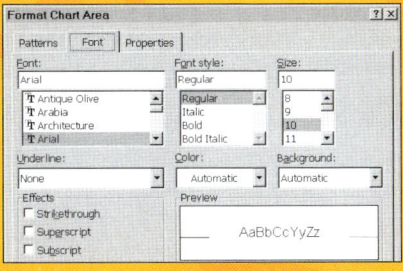

2. Click on the word Font and choose a font from the font list. Choose a style and size of font from the other lists. Then, click on the word Patterns.

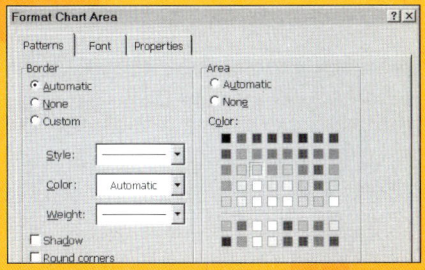

3. A selection of colours appears to the right. Click on a colour for the background of the chart box. Your choice appears in the Sample box.

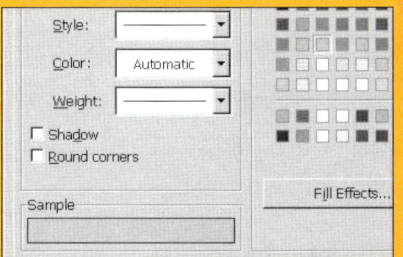

4. To add a border around the chart box, click on the Style, Color and Weight boxes. You can choose a style from each of the menus that drop down.

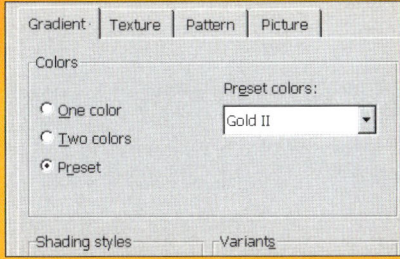

5. For a patterned background, click on the words, Fill Effects. Click on Gradient, then try clicking on some of the shading styles.

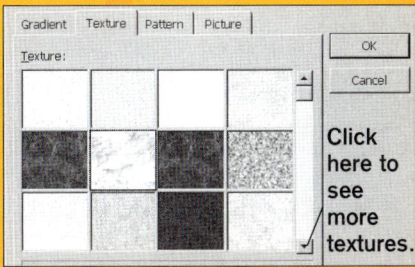

6. To see more styles, click on Texture or Pattern. When you've chosen a style, click on OK. Click on OK on the Format Chart Area box too.

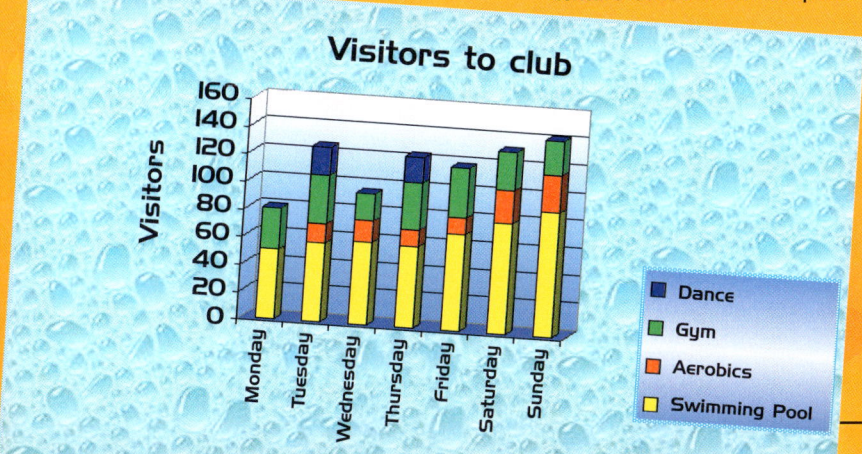

The background of this chart is a texture called Water droplets.

More changes

To change other parts of the chart, move the pointer over the part that you want to change. To select that part, right-click so black squares appear around it. On the menu that appears, click on the Format option, then follow steps 2-6 above. You can move selected areas in the same way as you move the chart box.

28. Finishing touches

You may have noticed that letters always appear to the left-hand side of a cell and that numbers always appear to the right. This page shows you how to position words and numbers exactly where you want them on your spreadsheet. You can also find out how to add a heading and make it appear in the middle of your work.

alignment tools

Align Right tool

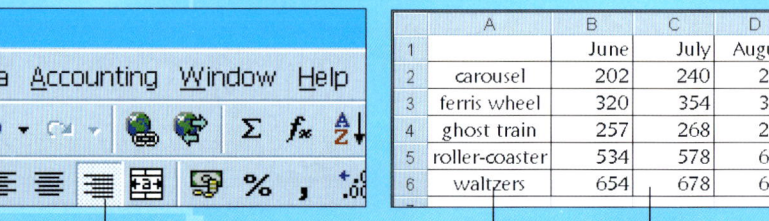

These cells are centred.   All these cells are aligned to the right.

1. Select the cells that contain the words or numbers that you want to adjust. Then, look on the toolbar for the three alignment tools.

2. Click on the Align Right tool. The words in the selected cells move to the right. The Align Right tool now looks like a pressed-in button.

3. Select some more cells and try clicking on the Align Left or Center tools. When you are happy with the way your spreadsheet looks, save it.

Adding a heading

This section shows you how to add a heading to your spreadsheet and make it appear across the top of several columns.

1. Move the pointer over the number 1 at the end of row 1. Click the right mouse button. On the menu that appears, click on Insert.

2. A new row appears above row 1. Click in the new A1 and type a heading. Press Enter. Select the cells in row 1, above the columns you've typed in.

Merge and Center tool

3. Click on the Merge and Center tool, beside the alignment tools. The heading you typed will move to the middle of the selected cells.

4. Click on the Align Left or the Align Right tool to move the heading to the left or the right. If you like, you can change the style of the heading too.

Tips

You can insert columns or rows anywhere on your spreadsheet, except where you've merged cells. You can remove them too.

1. To insert a column right-click on the letter at the top of the column. Click on Insert. A new column appears to the left of the one you clicked on.

2. To remove a row or column, right-click on either the row number or column letter. On the menu that appears, click on Delete.

29. Check your spelling

Microsoft® Excel 97 has a Spelling tool that can correct spelling mistakes that you make. You can use it to correct a whole spreadsheet, or you can check just one word. This page shows you how.

Getting Excel to check your spelling could save you time.

This is the Spelling box.

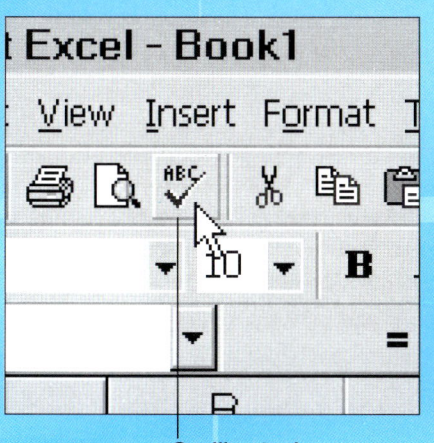

Spelling tool

1. To check the whole of your spreadsheet, first click on cell A1. Click on the Spelling tool on the toolbar. The Spelling box (see right) appears.

2. At the top of the Spelling box, you will see the first word on your spreadsheet that Excel doesn't recognize. Below it, you'll see a list of suggestions.

3. To change your word to one of the suggestions, click on the one you want, then on Change. If you don't want to change your word, click on Ignore.

4. Microsoft® Excel 97 will find all the words it doesn't recognize, then a message will tell you when the spell check is complete. Click on OK.

Select one word

The pointer changes shape.

1. If there is just one word you are not sure about, you can select just that word. Double-click in that cell. Move the pointer in front of the word.

2. Hold down the mouse button and move the pointer across the word to highlight it, then release. Follow steps 1-3 in the section above.

Tip

Microsoft® Excel 97 can get things wrong. It will try to correct words that it doesn't recognize, even though these may be correct (people's names, for example). Some words have two spellings (for example two and too) – Excel won't spot it if you get the wrong one. It is a good idea to check your work yourself too, just to make sure there aren't any more mistakes.

Switching off your computer

When you want to switch off your computer, you shouldn't just press the power button, like you can on other electrical equipment. First, you should close the Microsoft® Excel 97 program, then follow a simple process called **shutting down**, described on these pages. The opposite page shows you how to reopen the spreadsheets that you have saved.

Closing a spreadsheet

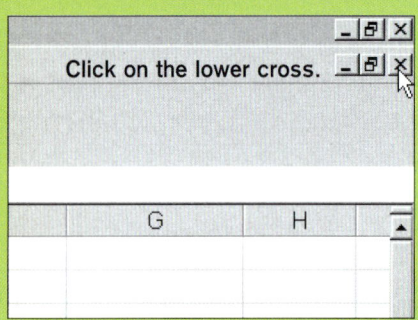

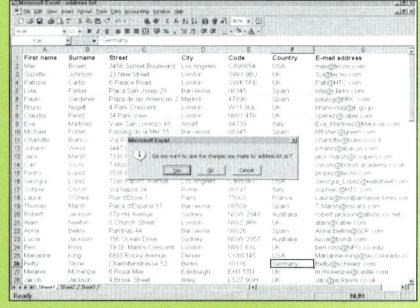

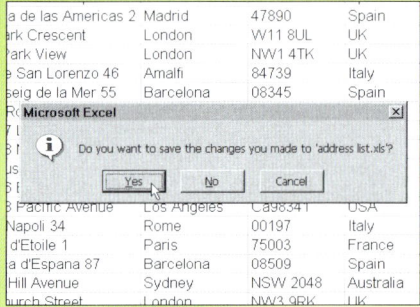

1. Press the Enter key to remove the insertion point from the screen. Then click on the lower cross in the top right-hand corner of the screen.

2. If you have made any changes to your work that you haven't saved, a message appears asking if you want to save these changes.

3. Click on Yes. The changes are saved and the spreadsheet closes. If you haven't saved this spreadsheet yet, the Save As box appears (see page 14).

Shutting down

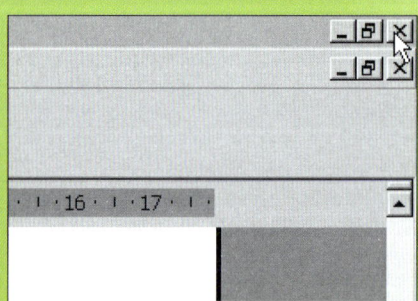

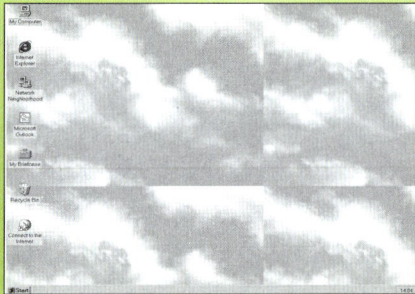

1. To close Microsoft® Excel 97, click on the remaining cross, in the top right-hand corner of the screen. The Microsoft® Excel screen disappears.

2. If there are any other programs open on your computer, close them by clicking on the cross in the top right-hand corner.

3. Now you will see the Microsoft® Windows® screen (see above) that you saw when you switched on your computer.

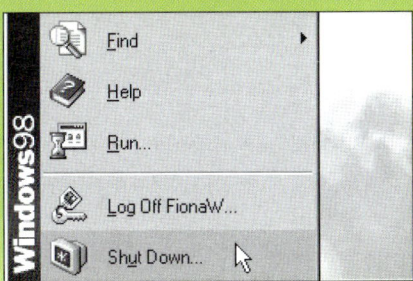
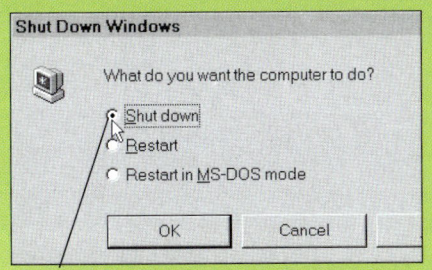
Click here so a black dot appears.

Press the power button on your monitor if it has one.

4. Click on Start, in the bottom corner of the screen, so that a menu appears. Move the pointer up the menu so Shut Down is highlighted, then click.

5. A box will appear in the middle of the screen. Click on the white circle beside the words Shut down. Then click on OK.

6. When your screen stops changing, your system unit will either switch off automatically or you will have to press the power button to switch it off.

30. Reopening a spreadsheet

These steps show you how to reopen any spreadsheet you have saved. If you have switched off your computer, switch it on again. Follow the steps on pages 5-7 to open Excel.

Open tool

The Open box
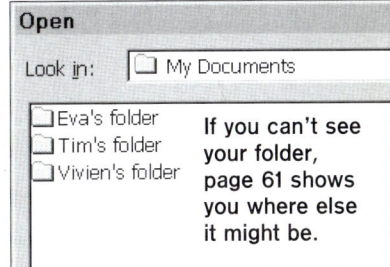

If you can't see your folder, page 61 shows you where else it might be.

1. Click on the Open tool on the toolbar. The Open box (see right) pops up on your screen. The Open box looks a bit like the Save As box.

2. If My Documents is in the Look in part of the box, your folder will be in the big, white area. Click on your folder, then on Open.

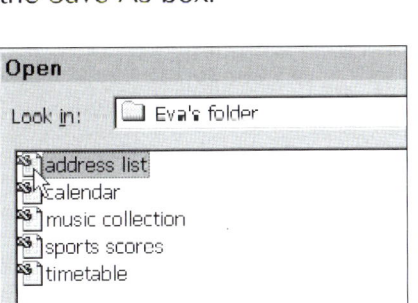
These are the names of the spreadsheets in your folder.

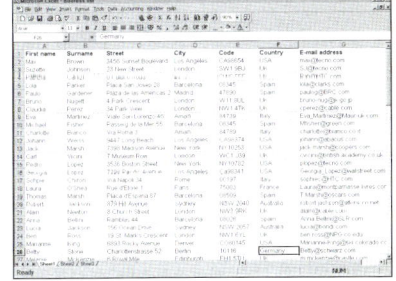

3. When your folder is in the Look in part of the box, you will see the names of any spreadsheets you have saved in the big, white area.

4. Click on the symbol beside the spreadsheet that you want to open so its name is highlighted. Click on Open at the right-hand side of the box.

5. Your spreadsheet appears on the screen just as you saved it. If you make any more changes to it, remember to save them.

Installing Microsoft® Excel 97

If Excel isn't on your computer, you'll need to **install**, or load, it. When you buy Microsoft® Excel, either on its own or as part of Microsoft® Office 97, you are given a disc, called a CD-ROM, and some instructions. On these pages, Excel has been installed as part of Microsoft® Office 97 Small Business Edition.

When you have closed all programs, the Windows® screen appears.

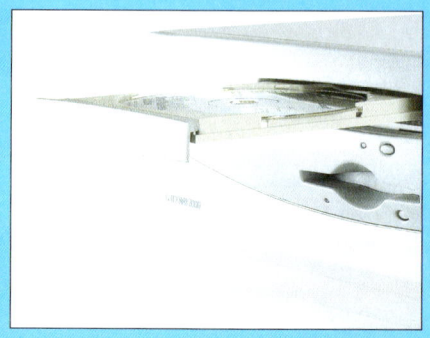

If you have a different edition of Microsoft® Office 97 or if you have Excel on its own, you may see slightly different things on your screen.

1. Before you start, close any programs you've been using. Find the CD-ROM drive on the system unit (see page 4), and press the button near the drive.

2. A drawer slides out. Place the CD-ROM in the drawer, with the writing facing up, and press the button again to close the drawer. Wait for a moment.

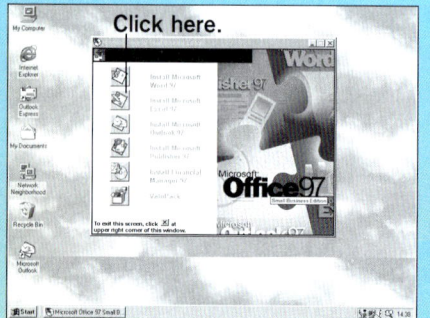

Click here.

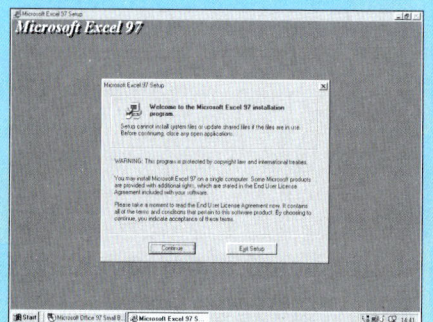

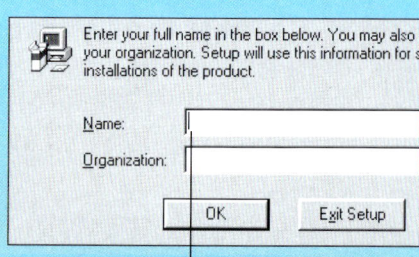

Your typing appears here. Press the Backspace key (see page 10) if you make a mistake.

3. You'll see the screen above, or one similar to it. Move the pointer over the square beside Install Microsoft® Excel 97, or Microsoft Excel® 97.

4. Click the left mouse button. When the above box appears, read the writing in it. This gives you information about Microsoft®. Click on Continue.

5. At the top of the next box, shown above, type your name and click on OK. Another box appears, showing your name. Click on OK.

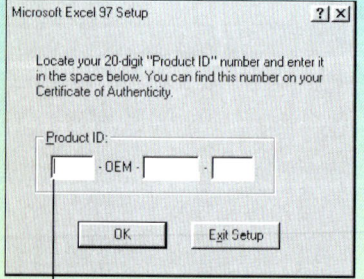

The Product ID number appears in the three white areas.

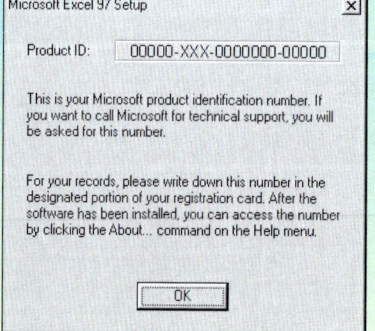

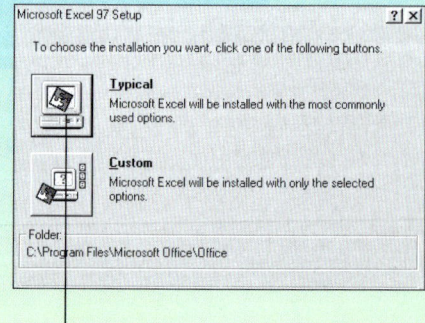

Click here.

6. This box appears. Find the Product ID number on the cover of the CD-ROM, and type it in carefully. The number will appear across all three boxes.

7. Click on OK. A box appears, confirming your number. Make a note of it, and keep it in a safe place. Now click on OK and wait.

8. A message tells you that Excel will go on your hard disk drive. Click on OK. Wait until another box appears. Click on the square next to Typical.

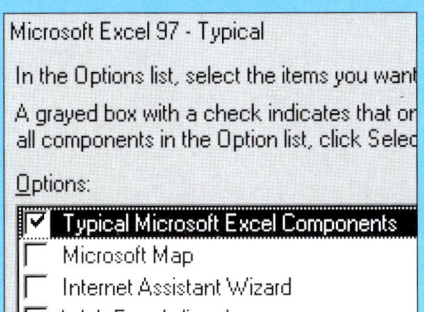

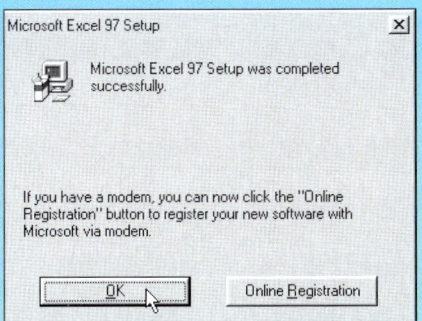

Click here to have a British English dictionary.

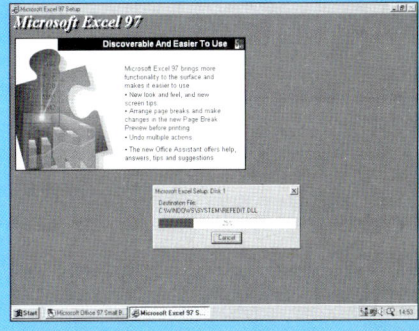

9. You will now be asked to confirm that you want to install the Typical parts of Microsoft® Excel 97. To do this, click on the word Continue.

10. The box, shown above, asks you which kind of dictionary you want. Choose one and click on that option. Then click on OK.

11. Wait until two boxes appear. A bar slowly moves across the white area of the smaller box. This may take a while. When it fills the box, Excel is installed.

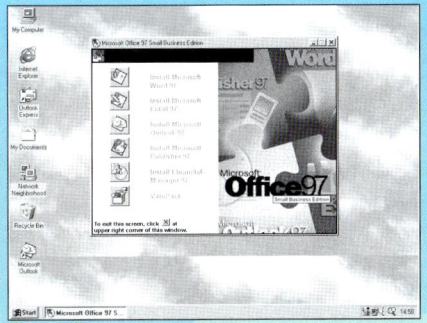

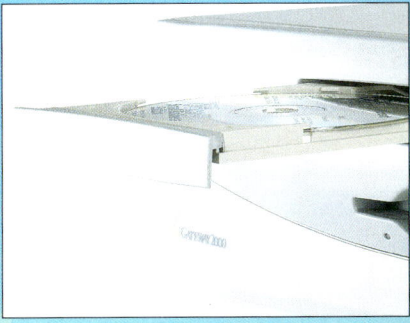

12. The above box tells you that you have successfully installed Microsoft® Excel 97. Now click on OK, to make the box disappear.

13. On the screen, you'll see the first installing screen again. Click on the cross in the top right-hand corner of the box to see the Windows® screen.

14. Finally, take the CD-ROM out of the drawer, put it back in its cover, and keep it safe. To open Microsoft® Excel 97, follow the steps on pages 6-7.

After installing

Once you've installed Microsoft® Excel 97, you're ready to start using Excel, and ready to start using this book. However, you will need to fill in your Registration Card, which is in the Microsoft® Office 97 box. When you've filled it in, send it to Microsoft®, to let them know that you've installed Excel on your computer. You'll find the Microsoft® address for your country in one of the leaflets in the software box.

Tip

As you're installing Microsoft® Excel 97, you may have to wait for a while before each new screen appears. This is quite normal – the computer's got a lot to do. You may also find that your computer switches itself off and back on again. Don't worry if this happens – just wait and watch.

59

Troubleshooting

If something unexpected happens while you are using your computer, there is probably a simple solution. Don't worry – it is very difficult to "break" a computer! Here are some tips on solving common problems.

General troubleshooting tips

1. When you switch on, your computer may ask you to type a password. If you don't know the password, ask someone else who uses the computer. Use the keyboard to type it in, then press the Enter key.

2. If you can't see Start, try moving the pointer to the very bottom of the screen, so that it becomes a tiny black arrow. Start should appear.

Click here, to make Excel fill the screen.

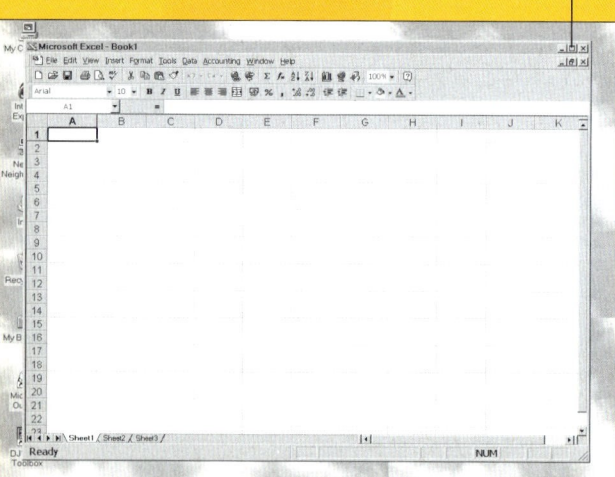

3. If Microsoft® Excel 97 only fills part of your screen, you can make it bigger by clicking on the Maximize tool, in the top right-hand corner of the screen.

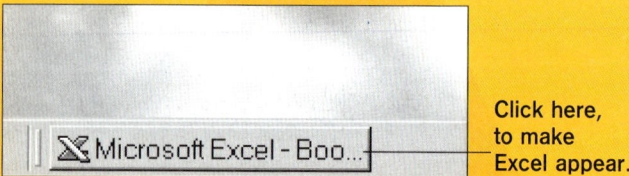

Click here, to make Excel appear.

4. If you can't see the Excel screen, it doesn't mean it isn't open. If it is open, there will be a rectangle at the bottom of the screen. Click on it to make the Microsoft® Excel 97 screen appear.

5. If your screen looks different from the one in this book, click on the word View, at the top of the Excel screen, then on Normal. The appearance of the screen changes.

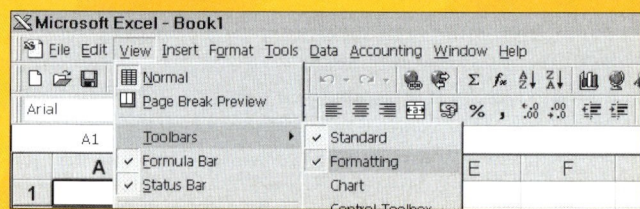

6. If you can't see all the toolbars shown in this book, click on View. You will need to click on Formula Bar and Status Bar so there is a tick beside each. You also need to move the pointer over Toolbars so a second menu appears. Click so there is a tick beside Standard and Formatting.

7. If you can't see part of the spreadsheet you've been working on, click on the arrows at each end of the scroll bars (see pages 8 and 13). Your work will move back onto the screen.

8. If you think that you've lost a spreadsheet, it may just be hiding behind another one. Click on the word Window, at the top of the screen. At the bottom of the menu are the names of all the spreadsheets that are open. Find the one that you want, click on its name and it will appear.

9. If you click on a tool and nothing happens, it may be because the insertion point is still on the screen. Press Enter to remove the insertion point, then click on the tool again.

10. If you press a key or click the mouse button to give your computer an instruction and nothing happens, your computer has probably crashed – this means it has stopped working. Hold down the Ctrl key and the Alt key, then press Delete. Follow the instructions your computer gives you.

Looking for Microsoft® Excel 97

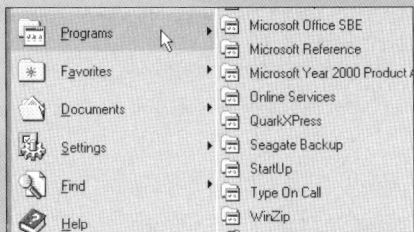

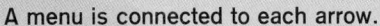
A menu is connected to each arrow.

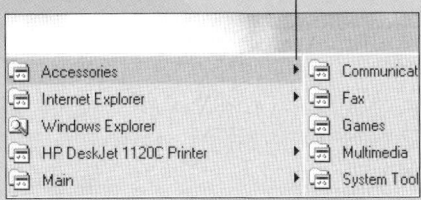

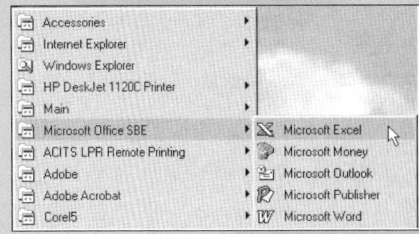

1. If you have clicked on Start, then on Programs, but can't find Excel on the second menu that appears, it may be hiding somewhere else.

2. Move the pointer over the first item on the second menu that has an arrow beside it and click. Another menu will appear. Look to see if Excel is there.

3. If you see Excel, click on it. If it's not there, click on each item on the menu with an arrow next to it. If you still can't find Excel, you'll need to install it.

Finding your folder

When you want to reopen a spreadsheet or save a spreadsheet, you may not always be able to find your folder in the Open box or in the Save As box. If you have used a different folder recently or someone else has used your computer, you may see other strange folders or symbols instead.

These steps show you how to find your folder in either the Open box or the Save As box.

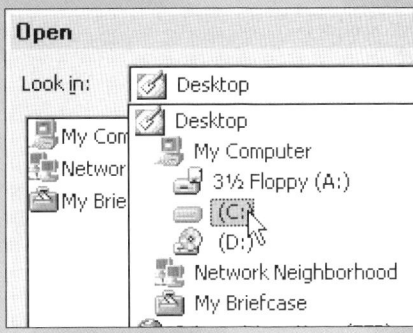

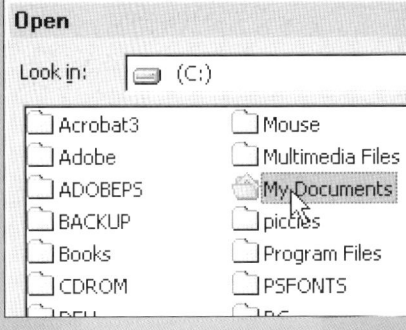

1. Click on the box beside Look in, or Save in, at the top of the Open or Save As box. On the list that appears, move the pointer over (C:), then click.

2. If My Documents isn't in the main part of the box, click on the arrows at each end of the scroll bar. Click on My Documents, then on Open.

Asking for help

If you are having trouble, Microsoft® Excel 97 has its own Help system, which you can try out. There are two ways of doing this. You can ask the Office Assistant for help or search through the Help index. When you've finished, click on the cross in the top right-hand corner of the Help box so it disappears.

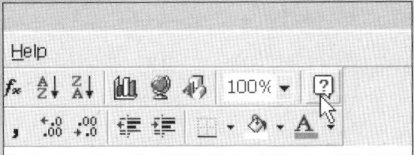

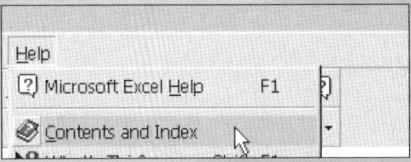

To use the Office Assistant, click on this tool. The Assistant appears, offering help. Type in a question, word or phrase, then click on Search.

To see the index, click on Help at the top of the screen, then on Contents and Index. Click on the Index tab, then follow the instructions that you see.

Shortcuts

As you use Microsoft® Excel 97, you may notice that there are several ways of doing the same thing – just use the way that you find easiest. Here are some alternatives that may help speed up what you're doing. The box at the bottom of this page gives a reminder of the keyboard shortcuts mentioned earlier in this book, as well as some new ones.

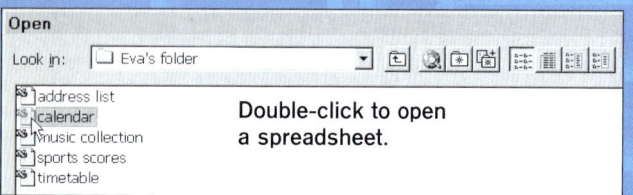

Double-click to open a spreadsheet.

When you want to open a spreadsheet using the Open box, first move the pointer over the symbol beside its name. Then double-click to open your spreadsheet. You can also double-click to open a folder.

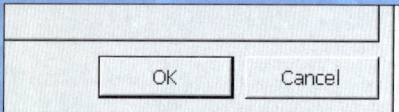

Instead of clicking on OK, you can just press Enter.

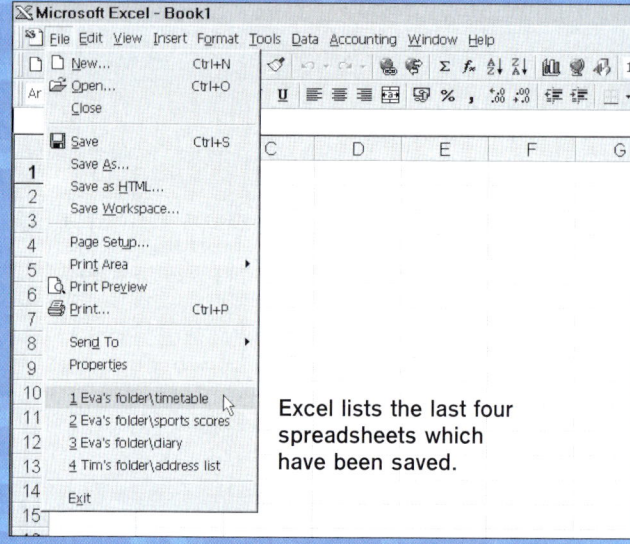

Excel lists the last four spreadsheets which have been saved.

When there is a box, such as the Format Cells box, on your screen, after you have chosen the options you want, you can just press Enter instead of clicking on OK. You can press Enter instead of clicking on the word Save, Open, Next or Finish on other boxes, too.

If you want to open a spreadsheet you have worked on recently, you don't need to use the Open box. Click on the word File, at the top of the screen. If you can see the name of the spreadsheet you want to open, near the bottom of the menu, click on it.

Ctrl + A	Selects the whole spreadsheet.
Ctrl + B	Makes the selected lettering bold.
Ctrl + C	Copies words that have been selected.
Ctrl + D	Deletes the lettering in the active cell.
Ctrl + I	Makes the selected lettering italic.
Ctrl + N	Creates a new spreadsheet.
Ctrl + O	The Open box appears.
Ctrl + P	The Print box appears.
Ctrl + S	Saves your work, if you've already named it. If you haven't named it, the Save As box will appear.
Ctrl + U	Underlines the selected lettering.
Ctrl + V	Pastes a cut or copied section in the active cell.
Ctrl + W	Closes your spreadsheet.
Ctrl + X	Cuts or removes words that have been selected.
Ctrl + Z	Undoes the last thing you did.

Computer words

Here are some of the computer words used in this book, with translations into everyday language. Words in italic lettering are explained elsewhere on this list.

The **active cell** is the *cell* with a thick line around it. Anything you type appears in the active cell.

AutoSum is the name of the tool you use to add a list of numbers.

A **CD-ROM** is a kind of disc that can transfer *programs* onto a computer.

A **cell** is a single box on a *spreadsheet*.

The **Chart Wizard** is a series of boxes that appear on your screen to help you create a chart or a graph.

Clicking is pressing down and releasing one of the buttons on the mouse, usually the left button.

You **close** a spreadsheet when you have finished working on it and you have saved it in a *folder*.

Columns are the vertical lines of cells on a spreadsheet.

When you **copy** something, your computer remembers it so you can *paste* it somewhere else.

When you **cut** something, you remove it. The computer remembers it so you can *paste* it somewhere else.

When you **delete** something you remove it completely from the spreadsheet.

Double-clicking is pressing and releasing the left mouse button twice, very quickly.

Excel 97 is the name of a spreadsheets program made by the company Microsoft®.

When you *save* spreadsheets, your computer calls them **files**.

A **folder** is where you store spreadsheets, or *files*.

A **font** is a style of lettering.

A **formula** is set of instructions that you can type to tell your computer to do calculations.

The **formula bar** is a box above your spreadsheet. The lettering or *formulas* in the active cell appear here.

A **function** is a set of instructions that Microsoft® Excel 97 has already prepared. Functions do different calculations, such as finding an average.

The **hard disk drive** is the part of your computer that stores information.

Hardware is computer equipment that makes up your *PC*.

When you **highlight** lettering, it appears on a dark background.

The **insertion point** is a small, flashing, vertical line, which shows you where your typing will appear.

When you **install** software, you load it onto a computer, by transferring information from a *CD-ROM* onto the *hard disk drive*. Once this is done, the information stays there for you to use.

A **menu** offers you a list of options to choose from.

My Documents is a ready-made *folder* on your computer. You can store your spreadsheets here.

When you **paste** something, you make *cut* or *copied* cells reappear in the active cell.

A **PC** (personal computer) is the kind of computer that is usually used in homes and offices.

The **pointer** moves around your screen as you move the mouse. It is usually an arrow or a cross shape, but can change into other shapes too.

Programs give computers instructions. Excel is a program, whereas Microsoft® Office 97 is a group of programs.

Rows are the horizontal lines of cells on a spreadsheet.

Saving is storing a spreadsheet on a computer.

You click on the arrows at each end of the **scroll bars** to see different parts of a spreadsheet.

When you **select** lettering, it appears on a dark background (see *highlight*). Selected charts have eight tiny black squares around them.

Shutting down refers to the steps that a computer needs to take before you switch it off.

Software is another name for computer *programs*.

When you use Excel, you work on a **spreadsheet**, or worksheet. This is a grid that can be used for calculating, organising and presenting information.

You click on **tools** to give your computer instructions. Tools are usually arranged on *toolbars*.

Toolbars are lines of *tools* that are grouped together.

Index

active cell, 9, 10, 16, 63
adding,
    a list of numbers, 23, 26
    using a formula, 20-21, 22, 29
alignment, 39, 54
alphabetical order, sorting into, 3, 41
arrow keys, 10, 16
axes, 46
AutoFilter, 42, 43
AutoSum, 26, 63
average, finding an, 32-33
backgrounds, 51, 53
bold lettering, 48, 62
borders, 50, 53
capital letters, 10, 11
CD-ROM,
    discs, 4, 58, 59, 63
    drive, 4, 58, 59
cells, 8, 16, 21, 36, 37, 38, 39, 50, 51, 63
charts, 44-45, 46-47, 52-53, 63
    adding labels and percentages, 45
    changing size, 52
    changing styles, 53
    Chart Wizard, 44-45, 46-47, 63
    column chart, 44, 46-47
    line graph, 3, 44, 47
    moving, 52
    pie chart, 3, 44-45
    printing, 52
    updating, 52
clicking, 6, 63
closing Excel, 56
closing spreadsheets, 56, 62, 63
columns, 8, 63
    adding the numbers in, 26
    deleting, 17, 54
    inserting, 54
    seeing more, 13, 18
    selecting, 17, 23
    widening, 12, 38
computer, PC, 4, 5, 56, 57, 60, 63
coordinates, 8, 21, 28, 30, 31, 32,
copying, 36, 37, 62, 63
corrections, making, 16-17
currencies, 24, 25, 26
cutting, 36, 37, 62, 63
dates, 34, 35, 38
decimals, typing, 24, 25, 26, 31, 33
Decrease Decimal tool, 33
deleting, 10, 62, 63
    lettering, 12, 16, 17,
    rows and columns, 54
double-clicking, 12, 16, 63
Excel 97 (Microsoft®), 2, 3, 4, 55, 63
    closing, 56
    installing, 4, 58-59, 61, 63
    looking for, 6, 60, 61
    opening, 6-7
    screen, 7, 8, 60
file, 15, 63
Fill Color tool, 51
filtering a list, 42-43
fitting more lettering in a cell, 12, 38-39

folder, 14, 15, 63
    creating a new, 14
    finding your, 61
    My Documents, 14, 57, 61, 63
    opening a, 15, 57
fonts, 49, 53, 63
    size, 49, 53
Format Cells box, 25, 35, 39
formula, 21, 63
    adding two numbers, 20-21
    AutoSum, 26, 63
    dividing numbers, 31
    multiplying two numbers, 30
    repeating a, 22, 29
    subtracting numbers, 28
formula bar, 9, 22, 63
function, 32, 63
hard disk drive, 4, 14, 63
hardware, 4, 63
headings, 12, 54
Help index, 61
highlighting, 6, 14, 55, 63
inserting rows and columns, 54
insertion point, 9, 11, 16, 63
    moving, 11, 16
    removing, 60
installing Microsoft® Excel 97, 4, 58-59, 61, 63
italic lettering, 48, 62
keyboard, 4, 5, 9, 10-11
legend, 45, 46
lettering,
    changing size, 49
    changing appearance, 48-49, 53
    copying, 36-37, 62, 63
    cutting, 36-37, 62, 63
    deleting, 12, 16-17
    fitting more in a cell, 12, 38-39
    pasting, 36-37, 62, 63
    selecting, 17, 55, 63
    typing, 9, 10, 11
lines,
    grid, 7, 8, 18, 21
    of lettering in a cell, 38-39
list, 24, 26
    changing numbers in a, 27
    filtering a, 42-43
    sorting a, 3, 40-41
menu, 6, 19, 25, 27, 61, 63
Merge and Center tool, 54
Microsoft®,
    Excel 97, 2-3, 4, 6, 7, 8, 55, 56, 58-59, 60, 61, 63
    Office 97, 4, 58, 59, 63
    Windows® 95 or 98, 4, 56, 58, 59
monitor, 4, 5
mouse, 4, 5, 6
moving,
    cells, 36, 37
    charts, 52
My Documents, 14, 57, 61, 63
New tool, 20
numerical order, sorting into, 40
Office Assistant, 9, 61

Open box, 57, 61, 62
pasting, 36, 37, 62, 63
PC (personal computer), 4, 5, 56, 57, 63
pointer, 6, 7, 22, 38, 52, 55, 63
Print Preview, 18
printer, 4, 5, 18
printing, 18-19, 51, 52, 62
programs, 2, 4, 7, 56, 63
reopening spreadsheets, 57, 61, 62
repeating a formula, 22, 29
rounding up numbers, 33
rows, 8, 63
    adding the numbers in, 22, 26
    changing height, 39
    deleting, 17, 54
    inserting, 54
    selecting, 17
    using more, 13
saving, 13, 14-15, 63
    in new folder, 15
    saving again, 15, 17
    saving new version, 27
screen,
    appearance, 3, 7, 8, 60
    clearing, 12
    seeing other parts of, scrolling, 13
    Microsoft® Excel 97, 7, 8, 60
    Microsoft® Windows®, 5, 56, 58, 59
scrolling, 8, 13, 60, 63
selecting, 17, 62, 63
    areas of cells, 17, 23, 25, 28, 44, 48, 49
    charts, 52
    one word, 55
    parts of a chart, 53
sequences, typing, 34
shortcuts, 62
    using Ctrl key, 15, 19, 37, 62
shutting down, 56, 63
software, 4, 63
    installing, 58-59
sorting, lists, 40-41
spelling checks, 55
spreadsheet, 2, 3, 7, 8, 13, 63
    closing, 56, 62, 63
    finding a closed, 57, 61, 62
    finding a missing, 60
    starting a new, 20, 62
Start, 6, 57, 60
sums, 3, 20, 22, 23, 32
switching on and off, 5, 56-57
times,
    changing the look of, 35
    typing sequences of, 34
tools, 8, 60, 63
toolbars, 8, 60, 63
typing,
    lettering, 9, 10, 11
    sequences, 34
underline lettering, 48, 62
undo, 17, 62
widening columns, 12, 38
worksheet (see spreadsheet), 8
Wrap text, 39

Acknowledgements

With thanks to Vivien Patchett and Cathy Wickens.
Microsoft® Excel 97, Microsoft® Office 97, Microsoft® Windows® 95 and Microsoft® Windows® 98 are either registered trademarks or trademarks of Microsoft Corporation in the United States and/or other countries. Product images, icon images and screen shots of Microsoft products reprinted with permission of Microsoft Corporation. This book is not a product of Microsoft Corporation.
Photographs of computers with permission from Gateway. Photographs of printers with permission from Hewlett-Packard Ltd.
Every effort has been made to trace the copyright holders of the material in this book. If any rights have been omitted, the publishers offer their sincere apologies and will rectify this in any future editions.

First published in 2000 by Usborne Publishing Ltd., Usborne House, 83-85 Saffron Hill, London EC1N 8RT, England. www.usborne.com Copyright © 2000 Usborne Publishing Ltd. The name Usborne and the device ☺ are Trade Marks of Usborne Publishing Ltd. All rights reserved. No part of this publication may be reproduced, stored in a retrieval system or transmitted in any form or by any means, electronic, mechanical, photocopying, recording or otherwise without the prior permission of the publisher. Printed in Spain.